The Significance of

Sri Ramakrishna's Life and Message

In The Present Age

with

THE AUTHOR'S REMINISCENCES
OF HOLY MOTHER
AND SOME DIRECT DISCIPLES

by Swami Satprakashananda

(Author of *Methods of Knowledge, Hinduism and Christianity,*
and other Vedantic treatises)

VEDANTA SOCIETY OF ST. LOUIS
1976

CONTENTS

PREFACE

One day in the house of Jatin Babu, who invited Swami Vivekananda to Dacca in 1901, I met my college professor of Sanskrit, Sashi Mohan Basak. In course of conversation Sashi Babu said, "When Swami Vivekananda returned to Calcutta the first time after preaching Vedanta in the Western world, his close relative Ramchandra Datta, a staunch devotee of Sri Ramakrishna, took him to task saying, 'Well, Ville [the nickname of Swami Vivekananda], you went to the Western world and all the time you harped on Vedanta. Why did you not preach Sri Ramakrishna, whose very name is conducive to man's liberation?'

"Swami Vivekananda replied, 'Well, if I talked to them about Sri Ramakrishna they would at once reply, "We have our Jesus Christ, what more have you to say?" Now I have preached to them the religion and philosophy of Vedanta and the Vedantic ideal of God-realization. Naturally they would inquire, "Who is the man who has realized the ideal in this age?" ' "

Vedanta Society   Satprakashananda
of St. Louis
August 27, 1975

Part I

THE SIGNIFICANCE OF
SRI RAMAKRISHNA'S LIFE AND MESSAGE
IN THE PRESENT AGE

CHAPTER I

SRI RAMAKRISHNA: HIS DIVINE LIFE
AND MISSION

Sri Ramakrishna was born in a village of idyllic beauty called Kamarpukur, about seventy-five miles northwest of Calcutta. This God-man of the nineteenth century appeared in human form twelve minutes before sunrise on Wednesday, February 17, in the year 1836. He was born of Brahmin parents who were renowned for their piety and generosity. They were of high social standing, but of humble means. The first sixteen years of his life were spent in his parental home. In the seventeenth year he left Kamarpukur for Calcutta.

Sri Ramakrishna was a born lover of God. He longed for nothing but God. In his early years he used to associate with holy persons and other pilgrims who visited Kamarpukur, often resting at the house of the village landlord. Pilgrims came to Kamarpukur on their way to Puri to visit the temple Jagannath. Sri Ramakrishna served these holy persons and listened to their conversations, and was impressed by their pure spiritual lives. He used to listen with rapt attention to the discourses on different religious scriptures, particularly the *Bhagavatam.*

He also attended the religious plays depicting scenes from the life of Sri Krishna. He had such a retentive memory that what he heard once he could remember thoroughly. He organized dramas with his playmates, and enacted those very scenes in the mango grove of the village. He would perform the daily worship in his family's chapel, worshipping the presiding deity of the family. He helped his mother with her duties. Sometimes he would repair to the cremation grounds on the outskirts of the village, and there he would pour out his devotion in rapturous songs.

From all this one can guess that his formal education was limited. He learned reading and writing and a little arithmetic. He even said jokingly that the multiplication table would make him feel dizzy. However, Sri Ramakrishna was very intelligent, and had an excellent memory.

He was the fourth child in the family, two brothers and one sister preceding him. His eldest brother went to Calcutta, and to augment the slender income of the family, opened a Sanskrit school. He also would perform religious duties in family homes. He wanted Sri Ramakrishna to accompany him, and so Sri Ramakrishna went to Calcutta, but he told his brother frankly that his heart craved that education that would remove all darkness of his heart forever, which would illuminate his heart completely. He had found that many scholars well-versed in scriptural knowledge did not live the life that was expected of them. He said, "I do not care for your bread-winning education." However, he did help his brother in performing his religious duties.

About this time one of the wealthiest ladies of Calcutta, Rani Rasmani (*Rani* as a title means queen) founded a temple dedicated to the Divine Mother Kali. The other major temple on the grounds was dedicated to Vishnu.

Besides, there were twelve temples dedicated to twelve aspects of Shiva. The temple buildings with the surrounding grounds occupied about thirty acres on the eastern bank of the Ganges in a place called Dakshineswar. Sri Ramakrishna's brother was appointed priest for the worship of the Divine Mother, Kali, and later Sri Ramakrishna became his assistant. After coming to Calcutta he came to this temple compound at Dakshineswar.

From his nineteenth year almost to the end of his life, he lived there — about thirty years — with the exception of short intervals such as his marriage, his visits to Kamarpukur, and his pilgrimages. The practice of spiritual disciplines, one after another, the realization of God in various stages, and the sharing of his spiritual treasures with both the orthodox and the unorthodox — all took place on this site.

He lived in a very small room, which was next to a semicircular veranda from which he could see the Ganges. The temple compound is on the eastern side of the Ganges, and Sri Ramakrishna's room faced the Ganges. The whole spiritual drama of his life was enacted in this small room at Dakshineswar.

It was on the 31st of May in the year 1855 that the temple was dedicated, and not long after this Sri Ramakrishna took up the duty of worshipping the main deity of the temple-garden, Kali, the universal mother. As soon as Sri Ramakrishna began worshipping the Divine Mother, Kali, the question arose within him — "Is this stone image a reality — the Divine Spirit? If she is real, I want to see her as she is."

Sri Ramakrishna was unlike a modern man in almost every respect. From the description Romaine Rolland has given us we find that his physical features and his personal appearance were not very attractive; besides, he always lived a life of complete renunciation. Modern man stresses acquisition, not renunciation. When we think of his life he seems to be completely unlike a modern man, yet in one respect he was the most modern of all moderns — he approached God with a strictly scientific attitude. He thought, "If God be a reality, I must see Him."

Sri Ramakrishna did not accept any authority. This is not the age of authority. He did not rely on the words of the scriptures. He even refused to read the scriptures. He did not rely on the opinions of philosophers. He did not go to a teacher. He knocked at the gate of heaven. "Knock and it shall be opened to you," and the door was opened. He wanted to see the Divine Mother, and the Divine Mother actually revealed herself to him.

What did he see? He saw one effulgent ocean of consciousness, blissful, the surging billows covering the whole universe, and he perceived Kali, the Divine Mother, as the very embodiment of that Supreme Consciousness, the Reality that is all-pervading, and at the same time all-transcendent. After this experience, he wanted to see the Divine Mother as the embodiment of Supreme Consciousness at all times; and the Divine Mother actually assumed form, and was always with him. This experience in the waking state (not in samadhi) became so intense that he saw the Divine Mother in all forms.

One day he perceived that the Divine Mother was in a

cat; that Supreme Consciousness was immanent in the trees, in the houses, in the very utensils used for the worship. At that time the cat came and was meowing; Sri Ramakrishna offered the food that was intended for offering to the Divine Mother, to the cat. There was an uproar in the whole temple. The complaint reached the ears of the son-in-law of Rani Rasmani. The son-in-law, Mathuranath Biswas, was impressed by the loving devotion of Sri Ramakrishna, and he wrote, "Until I come, do not interfere with the Brahmin." When Mathur came with his mother-in-law, the Rani, they realized that Sri Ramakrishna had gone beyond the range of ritualistic devotion, and both were deeply impressed.

The life of devotion is classified under two heads: one is the ritualistic stage, the other is the stage of ardent devotion which goes beyond all rules and regulations. Sri Ramakrishna could not carry on the ritualistic worship any more. He saw the Divine Mother everywhere. He was in a state of divine inebriation. At that time the news reached his home village that he had become insane. How could people understand that divine intoxication?

Because his behavior was not normal, some of his relatives suggested that if he were married, his mind would become balanced. They looked for a bride, and a girl was chosen. Sri Ramakrishna consented to marry, but as soon as he was married he came back to Dakshineswar and forgot everything. His bride was six years old and Sri Ramakrishna was about twenty-three years old. (It was really a betrothal, because in Hindu society there is no romance, the marriage being arranged by the parents.)

Again Sri Ramakrishna plunged into his spiritual

striving and spiritual realization. At that time a woman adept in Tantric discipline came to Dakshineswar. She was clothed as a nun. When she saw Sri Ramakrishna she at once recognized that he was in a state of divine ecstasy. The Divine Incarnation, Sri Chaitanya, lived this way, sometimes in a state of complete samadhi, sometimes in a half-conscious state, but his face was always beaming with joy and his heart was full of wisdom. The woman saint declared that Sri Chaitanya was born again in another form. The news reached the son-in-law of the Rasmani, who arranged a conference of great scholars versed in the scriptures. They were convinced that Sri Ramakrishna was not an ordinary soul, but Divine Spirit incarnate in human form.

Sri Ramakrishna was not satisfied. He wanted to see God in many different aspects. Why? Because his life was intended to demonstrate to the world the efficacy of the various spiritual disciplines prevalent in different faiths. Bhairavi Brahmani, the woman Tantric adept, had a great inclination to train Sri Ramakrishna in the mysteries of the Tantric religion and philosophy. He was initiated into the various disciplines in Tantra, which looks upon the universe as the manifestation of Divine energy.

The Divinity has two distinct aspects — static and dynamic. This entire manifold is the manifestation of the dynamic aspect of reality. The static aspect, which is very calm and is called Shiva, holds the dynamic aspect, which is called Shakti. The whole universe is a play of Shiva and Shakti. The transcendental Reality forms the basis of this world of becoming, but is ever unaffected. In itself, this world of becoming does not explain the universe. The two together form the true explanation of the universe.

After finishing the Tantric courses, Sri Ramakrishna's attention was drawn to Vaishnavism. He had already practiced three distinct forms of Vaishnavism. According to Vaishnava psychology, God can be approached with different devotional attitudes. These attitudes include the relationship between the worshipper and the worshipped (e.g. the attitude between the servant and the Master, the attitude between the ruled and the ruler). Then there is another attitude — between friend and friend; also the attitude between the parent and the child — the worshipper being the parent, God being the child. There is the sweet attitude; the worshipper approaching the Lord as the sole Beloved.

Sri Ramakrishna had practiced all of these attitudes excepting the parental attitude, and the sweet attitude. At that time an adept came — and it seemed mysterious that these teachers came at exactly the right moment, as though to fulfill some divine plan — and Sri Ramakrishna was initiated into the parental attitude, the parental love for Divinity. He realized Sri Ramachandra as the Gopal Rama, as the child, Rama. God assumed form as a child; and Sri Ramakrishna realized from that experience that Rama, who was incarnate as the son of Dasaratha, is the all-pervading Spirit.

When the Divine Spirit assumes form it does not mean It is limited to that form, but that through a particular form God's grace, God's knowledge, God's freedom, God's power, purity, and love, become particularly manifest wherever He is. He is the indwelling Self in all. The question is in the manifestation. He chooses a particular human form for the special manifestation of His grace, of His love, of His purity, so that human beings can be fully convinced of the Reality of God, the love and grace of God, and the wisdom of God; otherwise, how can human beings ever be convinced?

In this world of dualities order and disorder coexist. If you say God has created many beautiful things, you will have to say God has created many kinds of ugliness. If God has created all the saints, who has created all the sinners? God is responsible for all this, but still, He is above all this. He chooses a particular human form through which Divine Love, Divine Grace, Divine Freedom, Divine Purity become especially manifest. There is no better manifestation of Divinity anywhere than these God-men. Sri Ramakrishna realized that the same one who was manifest as the son of Dasaratha, Rama, was the all-pervading Spirit, and He was at the same time especially manifest as the indwelling self of incarnate beings.

The Spirit is the omnipresent Being, but this manifestation differs in living creatures. It is only in living creatures that the Supreme Spirit, all-pervading, is manifest as consciousness, or sentiency. If there is any sentiency anywhere it is only in living beings. God is omnipresent, God is Supreme Consciousness, Pure Spirit, self-effulgent, distinct from matter in every respect; yet, His manifestation as consciousness is only in living beings, and of all living beings, it is in the human mind that consciousness is particularly manifest as self-awareness. Distinct self-awareness does not exist in the sub-human level. There is some awareness, but no pronounced individual consciousness.

So we find that the difference is in the manifestation of the omnipresent Being. That omnipresent Being chooses a particular form and especially reveals His power and love for human beings. Sri Ramakrishna realized that that Supreme Being is at the same time the indwelling Self, and He is the all-transcendent reality.

Under the instruction of the woman saint, Bhairavi Brahmani, he practiced the sweet attitude towards God. Many Christian saints have realized God as the sole Beloved and had a spiritual wedding with Him. This individual soul, the human being, is conceived as the female principle. In mystical devotional psychology, all individual souls have been conceived as the female principle and God as the sole male principle. Sri Ramakrishna realized this and had the vision of Sri Krishna. Sri Krishna merged in his personality. Sri Ramakrishna knew from direct experience that each of these disciplines, the various attitudes of the devotee towards God, are efficacious and actually lead to the Goal; also that all the disciplines recorded in the Tantras are effective, if they are rightly followed. In this way his experiences established the truth of the Tantras, and established the truth of the Vaishnava religion.

Then another great teacher came who was a non-dualistic Vedantist. His name was Totapuri. When he saw Sri Ramakrishna, he thought, "Yes, here is the man who can practice this nondualistic Vedanta." Sri Ramakrishna said to him, "My mother is living, and I am married." "Never mind," said Totapuri, "what you have already attained is enough to guarantee your success in this nondualistic approach."

Through the practice of Tantra, seeing the whole universe as the manifestation of the Divine Mother, Sri Ramakrishna had gone completely beyond body-consciousness. A person who is beyond body-consciousness cannot think of himself as a man or a woman. So Totapuri said, "That is the thing." That is the great requisite for the realization of the individual spirit as identical with Supreme Spirit. Totapuri knew himself as pure spirit, so he went without clothing. What can clothe the pure spirit? Clothing is necessary for the body, but with Sri Ramakrishna when he, too, went beyond body-consciousness, his clothing dropped very often. He was naked, and was not even aware of it.

Totapuri initiated Sri Ramakrishna one morning very early as is the custom according to Vedic rites. He wanted his pupil to concentrate his mind fully upon the nondual Brahman beyond all forms and features. But Sri Ramakrishna was so deeply devoted to the Divine Mother, worshipping and meditating on Her through form, that it was difficult for him to go beyond this form. Each time he tried to take his mind to the formless, featureless, impersonal absolute Reality, he failed; and he said, "I can't go beyond this." Then Totapuri touched his forehead with a sharp pebble, and said, "Concentrate your mind here." Sri Ramakrishna did so and immediately his ego-consciousness was merged in Supreme Consciousness and the entire universe was lost.

This universe is dependent upon our body-idea. The moment we recede from body-consciousness, as in dreams or in deep sleep, we are not aware of this universe. The ego persists in the waking state and is associated with this psychical system. It has some perception of this objective universe and of the psychical universe. But the moment the ego goes beyond them, as in the sleep state, what does it know? In the sleep state a person does not know whether he or she is a man or a woman, a teacher or a student. He does not know if he is an American or a Chinese. He does not know anything in the sleep state, because in that state this ego becomes merged elsewhere. There is no idea, no feeling, no memory, no imagination of any kind. All the features of the mind are lost in unspecified ignorance. The mind is in a featureless, causal state. Nothing is perceived because the ego, upon which all these diversities are centered, is lost. Something like this happens in samadhi also.

In sleep, this ego enters into unspecified ignorance; in samadhi, the ego enters into unspecified, formless, featureless consciousness. Instead of darkness, it enters into light, and that light removes all darkness, the roots of all weaknesses forever. When we enter into sleep, our ego-consciousness for the time being becomes merged in ignorance. When this ego-consciousness returns from that ignorance to what we call the normal state of consciousness, our weaknesses are not removed; all the roots of our weaknesses remain there. This is the whole difference.

Sri Ramakrishna succeeded in concentrating his mind on that featureless, formless Brahman, and his ego-consciousness completely merged in that Supreme Consciousness —the formless, featureless absolute being. Very few return from that experience. Sri Ramakrishna returned, but he did not return so easily. Totapuri, the teacher, was surprised that in such a short time he could have nirvikalpa samadhi, which is considered to be the very apex of spiritual realization. The first day, the second day, the third day passed. Totapuri knew a certain process to bring the mind back by the utterance of a sacred formula, a sacred word. He repeated that sacred mantra, and gradually Sri Ramakrishna's mind came back.

After this experience Sri Ramakrishna could not see any evil anywhere. Even the most ordinary things would appear as if something under a guise, as it were; consciousness guised even in an evil person. Sri Ramakrishna was in this state of experience for six months. He had very little consciousness of the external world. A holy man was at the temple of Dakshineswar at that time, and he would feed him just a little bit of food to keep his body alive.

Twelve long years passed. Sri Ramakrishna made pilgrimages to different parts of India. The Dakshineswar temple was the halting station for many pilgrims on their way to Puri — from northern India to southern India. (It is the custom of many holy persons to see the four main places of pilgrimages in the four extremities of India — one in the north, one in the extreme south, one in the extreme east, and one in the extreme west.) Sri Ramakrishna associated with these holy persons, and shared his knowledge with them. In this way he became acquainted with the philosophical systems, and the different doctrines.

Sri Ramakrishna had the conviction that his life had a divine purpose, that it was intended to demonstrate the truth of religion in this age, when human beings were steeped in materialism, in atheism, scepticism, and agnosticism. He came in a very dark age, spiritually speaking, though materially, one might say it was a very advanced age. People had scientific knowledge, but spiritually, it was one of the darkest ages in human history. He was convinced that his life had a purpose — that he was to establish in the first place the reality of God; secondly, to demonstrate the truths of the various spiritual disciplines. So he turned to Mohammedanism and was initiated by a Mohammedan teacher. For three days he meditated upon the sacred formula that was given him, and he realized God through this approach, also.

Later he turned to Christianity, listened to the reading of the Bible, and meditated upon Jesus Christ. He used to visit a wealthy man of Calcutta who had a garden house near the temple of Dakshineswar, and this person was interested in Christianity. He would read the Bible to Sri Ramakrishna. When Sri Ramakrishna's mind was absorbed in thought of Jesus Christ, he went to another garden-house. There he saw an oil painting of the Madonna holding the baby Jesus in her arms. All at once he saw a divine light which entered into him. He came back to Dakshineswar, completely absorbed in the thought of Jesus Christ. For the time being he forgot to go to a Hindu temple. During this period he had a vision of Jesus Christ.

In this way, from direct experience, he declared that different approaches to God are all true. They are needed for the different individualities; spiritual practice must be suited to the psychical constitution of the aspirants. God has many different forms and aspects, though essentially He is the impersonal absolute Being. That same absolute Being is the all-pervading spirit, the indwelling self in each and every individual, immanent in the universe — and at the same time He is all-transcendent. Sri Ramakrishna taught that this great truth underlies all the religions of the world.

CHAPTER II

SRI RAMAKRISHNA, THE GREAT MASTER

Great spiritual personalities do not actually belong to any particular country or race. They realize their unity in the all-encompassing Supreme Being that transcends all limitations. Naturally, they stand out as world figures adored by millions of human beings all over the world. Sri Ramakrishna's birthday is observed not only in many cities and villages of India, but also in different parts of the world by persons belonging to different nationalities and creeds.

His birthday was observed in a very humble way by his own devotees when he was alive. We find a very interesting account of this birthday in the *Gospel of Sri Ramakrishna*. It was observed in the year 1883 on the eleventh of March, which fell on Sunday. (In India the religious festivals are observed on the lunar day.) As far as I know from the account given by one of his direct disciples, Swami Adbhutananda, not more than 150 persons gathered on that occasion; by 1950, had you been at our headquarters at Belur Math, you would have seen at least 100,000 persons there. Those devotees who gathered there in 1883 to celebrate Sri Ramakrishna's birthday could hardly imagine that the time would come when his name would encircle the globe and his birthday would be observed in such distant places as St. Louis and Buenos Aires in the West. This very day of Sri Ramakrishna's birth, in the year 1836, marks a turning point in modern history. It was the beginning of the decline of materialism and the rise of spiritual idealism.

Sri Ramakrishna was born in an age in which materialism was running rampant. The civilized world was in the grip of materialistic and mechanistic views of the world — scepticism was the order of the day. When people were dreaming of the world bereft of all ideas of religion, Sri Ramakrishna sought nothing but God. He dived deep into the bosom of the unseen, explored the entire region and came out with the direct experience of Reality and said that God alone is real. When the human mind was sold to sense knowledge, when any belief in the suprasensuous reality was considered to be superstition, Sri Ramakrishna declared that God alone is real.

The age needed such a demonstration. His life is the greatest demonstration of the reality of God. In this age of atheism, agnosticism and scepticism, Sri Ramakrishna has made God real. This is his unique contribution to this age.

Sri Ramakrishna was unlike modern men in every respect. He never cared for his personal appearance. He was the perfect embodiment of renunciation. He worshipped his own wife as the very image of the Divine Mother and maintained that relationship. His wife also worshipped him as the Divine Master. Now, think of this! If a person can command such a respect from the wife, from whom you cannot conceal a single weakness — think of it! His very wife worshipped him throughout life as the Divine Master.

Sri Ramakrishna came to Calcutta at the age of seventeen to help his brother in the performance of some religious duties. Then at the age of twenty he became a priest for the worship of the Divine Mother, Kali. From that time on, his life was a continuous struggle for God-realization. He was not satisfied in realizing God in one particular aspect. Through prayer he realized the Divine Mother; he also wanted direct experience of the Divine Mother, not only in the state of samadhi. He wanted to see Her constantly.

And the Divine Mother actually was present to his eyes, objectively, and talked with him. Sri Ramakrishna's direct disciple, "M," Mahendranath Gupta, who recorded his daily conversations which are now published in the *Gospel of Sri Ramakrishna,* told me about this. One day I said to him, "Ramakrishna saw God, he saw the Divine Mother; just as indicated in the *Bhagavad Gita:* 'Anyone who approaches Me, in whatever way, I favor him in that very way.' That truth is demonstrated in the life of Sri Ramakrishna." Then "M" told me, "What do you say? Not just *seeing* God — *talking* with God, just as I am talking with you!"

For the last twelve years of his life Sri Ramakrishna disseminated spiritual ideals. He lived close to a city which had absorbed Western materialism more than any other city in India. He lived in a suburb of that city and persons highly educated in those days came to hear his teachings, and listened to him spellbound.

An account of Sri Ramakrishna was given by one of the great rationalists of the time. His name was Pratap Chandra Mazumdar, and he was a rationalist theologian of the Brahmo Samaj. (He came to America in the year 1893 to represent the Brahmo religion, a protestant wing of Hinduism, at the Parliament of Religions in Chicago.) From his own experience he writes about Sri Ramakrishna; how Sri Ramakrishna's life was a direct testimony to the fact of the existence of God. Also, Sri Ramakrishna's inner experience was proof of the realization of God. God is real and He can be realized. Both these truths were completely demonstrated before the eyes of many sceptics, agnostics and atheists.

This is the account written by Pratap Chandra Mazumdar. It came out in the Theistic Quarterly Review of Calcutta in October, 1879. It was, of course, written a little earlier.

"My mind is still floating in the luminous atmosphere which that wonderful man diffuses around him whenever and wherever he goes. My mind is not yet disenchanted of the mysterious and indefinable pathos which he pours into it whenever he meets me.

"What is there in common between him and me? I, a Europeanized, civilized, self-centered, semisceptical so-called educated reasoner, and he, a poor, illiterate, unpolished, half-idolatrous, friendless Hindu devotee? Why should I sit long hours to attend to him, I who have listened to Disraeli and Fawcett, Stanley and Max Muller, and a whole host of European scholars and divines? I who am an ardent disciple and follower of Christ, a friend and admirer of liberal-minded Christian missionaries and preachers, a devoted adherent and worker of the rationalistic Brahmo-Samaj — why should I be spell-bound to hear him?

"And it is not I only, but dozens like me who do the same. He has been interviewed and examined by many, crowds pour in to visit and talk with him. Some of our clever intellectual fools have found nothing in him, some of the contemptuous Christian missionaries would call him an impostor, or a self-deluded enthusiast. I have weighed their objections well, and what I write now, I write deliberately.

"The Hindu Saint is a man under forty. He is a Brahmana by caste, he is well-formed in body naturally, but the dreadful austerities through which his character has developed appear to have disordered his system. Yet, in the midst of this emaciation, his face retains a fullness, a child-like tenderness, a profound visible humbleness, an unspeakable sweetness of expression and a smile that I have seen on no other face that I can remember.

"Ramakrishna Paramahamsa (for that is the name of this saint) is the worshipper of no particular Hindu god. He is not a Saiva, he is not a Sakta, he is not a Vaishnava, he is not a Vedantist. Yet he is all these. He worships Siva, he worships Kali, he worships Rama, he worships Krishna, and is a confirmed advocate of Vedanta Doctrines. He accepts all the doctrines, all the embodiments, usages, and devotional practices of every religious cult. Each in turn is infallible to him. He is an idolator, yet is a faithful and most devoted meditator of the perfections of the one formless, infinite Deity whom he terms Akhanda Sachchidananda (Indivisible Existence-Knowledge-Bliss).

"Nor is his reverence confined within Hinduism. For long days he subjected himself to various disciplines to realize the Mohammedan idea of an all-powerful Allah. He let his beard grow, he fed himself on Moslem diet, he continually repeated sentences from the Koran. His reverence for Christ is deep and genuine. He bows his head at the name of Jesus, honours the doctrine of His sonship, and we believe he once or twice attended Christian places of worship. These ideas at all events show the catholic religious culture of this great Hindu saint.

"A living evidence of the depth and sweetness of Hindu religion is this good and holy man. He has wholly controlled his flesh. He is full of soul, full of the reality of religion, full of joy, full of blessed purity. As a Siddha Hindu ascetic he is a witness of the falsehood and emptiness of the world. His testimony appears to the profoundest heart of every Hindu. He has no other thought, no other occupation, no other relation, no other friend in his humble life than his God. That God is more than sufficient for him. His spotless holiness, his deep unspeakable blessedness, his unstudied, endless wisdom, his child-like peacefulness and affection towards all men, his consuming, all-absorbing love for God are his only reward.

"Then in the intensity of that burning love of God which is in his simple heart, the poor devotee's form and features suddenly grow stiff and motionless; unconsciousness overtakes him, his eyes lose their sight and tears trickle down his fixed, pale but smiling face. There is a transcendental sense and meaning in that unconsciousness. What he perceives and enjoys in his soul when he has lost all outward perception — who can say? Who will fathom the depth of that insensibility which the love of God produces.

"But that he sees something, hears and enjoys when he is dead to all the outward world, there is no doubt; but why should he in the midst of that unconsciousness burst into floods of tears and break out into prayers, songs and utterances, force and pathos of which pierce the hardest heart and bring tears to eyes that never wept before by the influence of religion."

Sri Ramakrishna's life and teachings stream into human consciousness, penetrating all religious and anti-religious ideas and views. With Sri Ramakrishna, in the words of Swami Turiyananda, religion was a matter of give and take — not a matter of words. If you went to Sri Ramakrishna, he could give you religion this way, not simply using words as we do, not giving out empty words, but something tangible. Swami Vivekananda says, "Who has ever heard of such a miracle as this humble priest performed every day under our very eyes. What is that miracle? Taking the human mind, or human nature, in the palm of his hand as a piece of dough and giving it any shape." Swami Vivekananda spoke from his own experience.

We know from what reports we have received how he transformed the life of Girish Chandra Ghosh, the great actor-dramatist of India; how he transformed the life of Girish's friend, Kali Pada Ghosh, and many others. Even persons who had no belief in God would be converted to Him by simple methods. Just through humor, he could transform lives.

I heard a report from Swami Turiyananda, that a man from Jubbulpur was in a state of great distress. Sri Ramakrishna, after hearing him, found that it seemed to be beyond human power to solve his problem. Sri Ramakrishna said:

"You do one thing, you pray to God. When all human power or earthly powers fail, there is nothing else to depend on but God. You pray to him."

"I have no belief in God," said the man.

"You don't believe in God?"

"No, I don't believe in God."

"You do one thing — can you say, 'if there be such a reality as God — O God, if there be such a God, will you help me, if you exist — or, if there be any God, let me be helped by Him, because I see no other way of getting out of this difficulty.' "

The man said, "Yes, this much I can do."

So the man went home and prayed, and actually found a way out of his peril. Later he came to Sri Ramakrishna and said, "My prayer is answered."

See, how he could transform human life!

The account of Kali Pada Ghosh also shows how he performed miracles. Kali Pada Ghosh used to drink very much and tyrannize his wife. His wife was helpless. In Hindu society there is no divorce. The only refuge is the parent's home. So the wife came to Dakshineswar. She met the Holy Mother and said to her:

"Mother, this is my situation. Can you help me?"

"You go to him, to the master," said the Holy Mother.

When she came to Sri Ramakrishna, he said, "Holy Mother will help you."

She came back to the Holy Mother. This time, the Holy Mother said, "Repeat the sacred mantram" (a sacred word she had given her). The woman began to repeat the mantram continuously.

One year passed, the second year also passed and the third year was about to be over when at last, one day, Kali Pada Ghosh came to see Sri Ramakrishna. He was scoffing at religion as usual. However, he sat down quietly and after listening to Sri Ramakrishna for some time, he got up.

"Well," said Sri Ramakrishna, "What is the matter?"

"I feel thirsty."

"We shall give you something to drink."

"No, no, I do not want any water, I want a real drink."

Sir Ramakrishna understood what Kali Pada wanted, so he said, "I shall give you a real drink."

"Do you really have such a drink? I do not want your country-made drink. I want British brandy."

"Sit down. What we have is very strong, you will not be able to bear it."

"Yes, that is what I want. That is what I want."

Then Sri Ramakrishna, who had been seated on the little cot, moved a little and touched Kali Pada. The moment he was touched, something happened within him. He began shedding tears. The man who had never wept for anybody in his life was shedding tears profusely and he could not resist it. Kali Pada Ghosh the sceptic was finished, and he became the devotee of all the disciples of Sri Ramakrishna throughout his life. Any follower of Sri Ramakrishna who came to Bombay would be his guest. (He was the manager of a British paper merchant's office there.)

We know also, how one day at Cossipore garden on the first of January, in the last year of his life, 1886, Sri Ramakrishna came down from his room. It was Sunday and about thirty devotees had gathered there. As Sri Ramakrishna was passing by a tree, Girish Chandra Ghosh, who was seated there with other devotees, came forward and bowed down to Sri Ramakrishna. Sri Ramakrishna said to him, "Girish, what have you found in me that you go to everybody and say all these things about me — that 'he [meaning himself] has divine power; he is an Incarnation of God.' "

"What can I say about Him whose glory the angels and the great Gods cannot exhaust," Girish replied. "What can I say about Him!"

As soon as Sri Ramakrishna heard this he was transported into a different spiritual realm. In that state he touched Girish. Others, also, came to him and he blessed them. All had a wonderful spiritual experience.*

Sri Ramakrishna had an exceptional mind and because

*See Appendix D for Swami Saradananda's account of this incident.

of that he was able to practice various religious courses. To practice one particular religious course and reach the goal is a life-long task which very few can fulfill. Rare are the personalities who can follow one particular course in this life and reach the goal. It was given to Sri Ramakrishna to practice one course after another and to reach the goal. And such was his power not only over his own mind but over the minds of others, that just by a touch, or simply by a look, by a word or by a wish he could transform human lives.

Sri Ramakrishna's message is very simple. God is real — not only real, He is the sole reality, because the reality of everything else depends on the reality of God. In the absolute sense, He alone exists. All other existences are dependent on Him. Through knowing this He can be realized. This is what he demonstrated. And God can be realized not by one particular way, but by any spiritual discipline provided you fulfill these two particular conditions — one, inner purity, and two, devotion to God. Fulfill these two conditions and follow any spiritual line that appeals to you and you will reach the goal — the realization of God. This is his great message in the present age.

What does this message do for us? This message makes life meaningful. There is a goal which is attainable and where there is an end to all human sufferings and bondages. There you can attain that eternal life which you are dreaming of, that absolute peace and freedom. Sri Ramakrishna demonstrated that. That goal makes this life in the world secure, because when you seek that ideal your moral life becomes sound. Your material life can never be sound unless your moral life is sound.

So, in this declaration, Sri Ramakrishna points out that your economic life, your social life, your aesthetic life can be secure only when you turn to the spiritual ideal. Otherwise, your moral life can reach the limit of enlightened self-interest and cannot go beyond that. Enlightened self-interest is too shallow for safety and security in this world. It is not unselfishness in the true sense.

Sri Ramakrishna again says that you can reach God by any of the religions of the world. So his message establishes harmony and peace among the different religions of the world. His message makes life meaningful, and it makes this life of progress safe and secure. This is his great contribution to the modern age. Though most unmodern in his way of living, he has given the greatest contribution that this modern age can have. So his birthday is actually a turning point in modern history.

Swami Vivekananda, in a lecture delivered in New York City, gave this account of the great Master:

"I heard of this man and I went to hear him. He looked just like an ordinary man with nothing remarkable about him. He used the most simple language, and I thought, can this man be a great teacher? However, I crept near to him and asked him the question which I had been asking others all my life: 'Do you believe in God, Sir?' 'Yes,' he replied. 'Can you prove it, Sir?' 'Yes.' 'How?' 'Because I see Him just as I see you here, only in a much intenser sense.' That impressed me at once.*

*Actually, Swami Vivekananda had, at that time, no faith in the nondualistic teaching that there is one reality immanent in the whole universe. But one day Sri Ramakrishna touched him and he found that all these finite things and beings were floating in one eternal abiding reality.

"For the first time I found a man who dared to say that he saw God, that religion was a reality, to be felt, to be sensed in an infinitely more intense way than we can sense the world. I began to go to that man, day after day, and I actually saw that religion could be given. One touch, one glance, can change a whole life. I have read about Buddha and Christ and Mohammed, about all those different luminaries of ancient times, how they would stand up and say, 'Be thou whole,' and the man became whole. I now found it to be true, and when I myself saw this man, all scepticism was brushed aside.

"It could be done, and my Master used to say: 'Religion can be given and taken more tangibly, more really than anything else in the world.' Be therefore spiritual first; have something to give, and then stand before the world and give it. Religion is not talk, or doctrines or theories, nor is it sectarianism. Religion cannot live in sects and societies. It is the relation between the soul and God; how can it be made into a society? It would then degenerate into business, and wherever there are business and business principles in religion, spirituality dies. Religion does not consist of erecting temples, or building churches, or attending public worship. It is not to be found in books, or in words, or in lectures, or its organizations. Religion consists in realization."

"The second idea that I learned from my Master, and which is perhaps the most vital, is the wonderful truth that the religions of the world are not contradictory or antagonistic. They are but various phases of One Eternal

Religion. That One Eternal Religion is applied to different planes of existence, is applied to the opinions of various minds and various races. There never was my religion or yours, my national religion or your national religion; there never existed many religions, there is only the one. One Infinite Religion existed all through eternity and will ever exist, and this Religion is expressing itself in various countries, in various ways. Therefore, we must respect all religions and we must try to accept them all as far as we can."[1]

[1] *The Complete Works of Swami Vivekananda,* Vol. IV, pp. 175, 176.

CHAPTER III

SRI RAMAKRISHNA: HIS RELATION
TO VEDANTA

A newcomer to Vedanta, who has a vague idea of Vedanta and also of the life and teaching of Sri Ramakrishna, may very well wonder why the Vedanta movement in America is associated with Sri Ramakrishna. What is the relationship between Sri Ramakrishna and Vedanta? Why does Sri Ramakrishna receive special adoration in all Vedanta Centers? His picture is installed at the altar. Evidently, there is a direct connection between the Vedanta movement in America and Sri Ramakrishna. It was a disciple of Sri Ramakrishna, Swami Vivekananda, who initiated this movement and it was Sri Ramakrishna who started the monastic Order consolidated by Swami Vivekananda; this Order worships Sri Ramakrishna as an Incarnation of God. Naturally, Sri Ramakrishna is adored by the Ramakrishna-Vedanta movement.

But that is not the reason why Sri Ramakrishna receives special worship at the Vedanta Centers in America. The main reason is — in the whole history of Vedanta Sri Ramakrishna is its most comprehensive representative. Vedanta is associated with him simply because he is the best exemplar of Vedantic ideals and Vedantic disciplines. In the history of India from very ancient times there have been countless sages and seers who have embodied one or another aspect of Vedanta, who have also preached one or another aspect of Vedanta. But Sri Ramakrishna illustrates the entire Vedanta. His life is the most complete demonstration of Vedantic truths and Vedantic practices.

In what way is Vedanta comprehensive? In this way — according to Vedanta there is one Supreme Being, without a second; it is absolute Being, absolute Consciousness, absolute Bliss. When an individual realizes *That,* he realizes Pure Consciousness, limitless, the very perfection of existence. But as long as an individual retains his "I" consciousness, he perceives this objective universe, physical and psychical.

At the same time, God is the ruler of the universe. He is the one precondition for the existence of the world, and also for the finite experiencer. Three things become simultaneously real —the individual experiencer, the world of experience, and their supreme Ruler who maintains all individuals and this manifoldness, as one connected whole. One cannot exist without the two others. But that is not the whole of reality. This is a relative existence. In a relative existence, one cannot be quite independent of those who are related. Beyond this relativity there is one absolute existence, and that is Supreme Brahman, impersonal, formless, featureless, without the distinction of attribute and substance, Pure Consciousness.

That Supreme Being is immanent in this manifoldness. He is not out of existence, He is penetrating everything. As long as we perceive this manifoldness, that supreme, transcendental being is the very self of the universe. He is the Supreme Self, the very basis and being of everything — even the worst. Vedanta declares this unequivocally, irrevocably.

You may or may not believe, you may or may not comprehend it: One Being, the innermost Reality, is the same in an atom as in a human being.

So that nondual Consciousness, one without a second, beyond all features and forms and distinctions, is the all-pervading Self of this manifoldness. He, the all-pervading Self, is not an inert existence. He controls the whole universe from within. He, who is the internal Ruler, who controls all laws, is at the same time the benign providence, and also the God of Love and Grace, leading bound souls to complete liberation. He is the Supreme Self, that impersonal absolute Being, beyond all distinctions and differences. Transcendental but immanent in this manifoldness, He is the all-mighty, omniscient Ruler of the universe — the all merciful Leader of all souls to complete freedom.

That Supreme Being is the indwelling Self in each and every living creature. This self-awareness is the central fact in your personality, the direct expression of that Supreme Reality. You discover the Reality in this universe by discovering your own Self. That is the central teaching of Vedanta. Consciousness is fundamental in this universe. Without presupposing Consciousness you cannot establish anything; you cannot affirm anything, you cannot deny anything. It is the one presupposition of each affirmation and each denial. How can you explain it away? In explaining it away, you have to acknowledge it. Without acknowledging Consciousness, how can you explain away something? That is the basic Reality, one ultimate presupposition of each and every kind of existence.

Vedanta recognizes one Supreme Being, and different

aspects of that Supreme Being. He is the Paramatman, the Supreme Self; He is Isvara, the Lord of the Universe; He is the Bhagavan, the God of Grace and Love. He is also this individual self — "The Kingdom of God is within you," says Jesus Christ. And that Supreme Being, formless, featureless, is full of blessed qualities in relation to this universe. We cannot conceive of God without reference to this manifoldness. Our human mind is so limited that whatever conception we have of God is always related to this universe, comprising the living and the non-living.

Just as there are many aspects of the Divine Being, so there are different forms of the Divine Being. The same benign Lord manifests Himself in forms — He assumes form. If a devotee worships Him through form, that form is not just his mental construction. The Lord Himself appears in that form! It is not just the imagination of the votary, it is actually the form in which the Lord manifests Himself. God can be realized in any of these aspects.

Vedanta does not hold the attitude of the agnostics, "Yes, God is, but He is unknown and unknowable." God has many aspects and He can be realized. The realization of God, which is the Supreme Ideal of life, which removes all darkness, all limitation, all imperfection, satisfies the innermost craving of man for complete freedom, for immortality, for complete blessedness. That is the one Supreme Ideal of each and every living creature. Every living being is progressively moving, directly or indirectly, rightly or wrongly, to this supreme culmination.

There are many ways to realize God in different aspects. An individual according to his capacity, his aptitude, and his condition in life, can choose a certain discipline suited to the ideal he conceives with regard to the Divine Being; and he can ultimately reach God. Disciplines vary: there is the path of work, the path of knowledge, the path of concentration. And there are many methods of worship — physical, verbal, mental. All these have their respective places in Vedantic spiritual culture. This is why we say Vedanta is very comprehensive, and this is why Vedanta looks upon all the different religions as so many pathways to the same Supreme Being.

According to Vedanta, religion is one; eternal, universal. The spiritual truths explicit in the different religions are the same though dogmas differ. Some religions are so overcrowded with doctrines and dogmas that their own followers do not know the basic spiritual truths. Vedanta takes a very firm stand on these basic truths. This is why in the eyes of Vedanta all the religions are so many pathways to the same goal. In accepting Vedanta we accept Christianity, at least in its essential aspect (not with every dogma, not with complete "churchianity"); we accept Mohammedanism; we accept Zoroastrianism, we accept Judaism — all the living religions. A Vedantist is a Christian at the same time because of our worship of Christ; he is a Buddhist at the same time because we worship Buddha. All the different religions are so many pathways to the same Supreme Goal.

This comprehensive note of Vedanta was actually experienced by Sri Ramakrishna and reaffirmed in this modern age. How did he reaffirm and verify this by his own experiences? The central theme in Vedanta is the realization of God. Religion does not rest just on belief, or just on assent to certain dogmas. Religion does not mean some kind of custom or form. Religion means realization. You are nowhere in spiritual life until you realize the Ideal. That was the dominant note in Sri Ramakrishna's life. He did not depend upon any authority and he was the most modern of all moderns in this respect. He did not even read the scriptures. Scriptures do not reveal God to you. You may consume an entire library of scriptures, and carry all the scriptures of the world in your head, still, God may be absent.

So, according to Vedanta, God has to be realized. One should not be satisfied just with scriptural study. Sri Ramakrishna knew that. He said, "I want direct perception of God — if He is real, let me see Him." The test of truth is direct experience. He did not depend upon philosophical discussion or speculative reason. He approached God directly.

At the age of twenty he became the priest for the worship of Kali. He became a worshipper of Kali, but he was not just that. As soon as he started the worship of Kali the question came to his mind — is this Kali just a stone image? Is there any reality beyond this image? If there is a reality, I must see that. Day and night there was no other concern for him excepting the direct perception of the truth beyond the image. Incessantly he prayed, incessantly he cried, pouring out his devotion in songs sung by the previous worshippers and devotees of Kali. At last, he had the vision — he had the perception of Kali, not only in form, but as Supreme Consciousness. When he saw the form he knew that this form was not just a stone image, but the very embodiment of Divine Consciousness, all-pervading.

He knew from the very beginning the truth that God is not limited in any form. He may manifest Himself in any form, but the form through which God manifests Himself is the very embodiment of Divine Consciousness. With reference to Kali, he always said: "*Mass of spirituality, mass of spiritual Consciousness* — not just a stone image. The form I see of Kali, appearing before me, is the form of the limitless Consciousness, the embodiment of spiritual Reality."

When through further spiritual practices he saw that form always, he was not even satisfied with that. He knew that the reality beyond this form has to be distinctly perceived, and he wanted to realize God in other aspects as well. There has never before been such a hungry soul! Most of the spiritual personalities of the world were satisfied with one or another aspect of God, and they completed their spiritual life with great difficulty and reached God; but there has not been another soul so far as we know, who was not satisfied with just one aspect of God, but wanted to realize God in many aspects.

After long years of disciplines, Sri Ramakrishna realized both the personal God and the impersonal, he saw the multiplicity and the unity at the same time.

From the year 1871, many educated and sophisticated people of Calcutta came to him, and Sri Ramakrishna's teaching began in a more formal way. He never gave a lecture. People came to him at any time. The door was always open, since the tropical climate in India permits it. Visitors came, asking him about God, and words of spiritual wisdom poured from his mouth. He gave spiritual truths, and at the same time was, off and on, in samadhi. Many modern persons, who could not think of samadhi as anything but a trance, or some kind of nervous derangement, or distortion, were impressed. Pratap Chandra Mazumdar, the leader of the Brahmo Samaj, testifies that when Sri Ramakrishna was in samadhi, his whole frame was radiant with light. His face was beaming with joy. Even the most sceptical-minded person could not but be impressed by the genuineness of the spiritual experience Sri Ramakrishna was having at that time. Even a photograph of him has caught that radiance.

I remember hearing Swami Shivananda, a direct disciple of Sri Ramakrishna, say, "From my childhood I wanted to know if God could be realized, and I was told that God is real and he could be experienced in a state of samadhi. It was my great desire to see somebody who had realized God in that state, and had that mystical experience." Swami Shivananda was told there was one person who lived at Dakshineswar who had actually realized God in samadhi.

The Swami had contacted another person who was said to have had samadhi, but it did not impress him at all, because there was some distortion in his face. He thought, "If this be samadhi, I have no respect for it." Swami Shivananda liked that person very much, had great admiration for him because of his other spiritual qualities. But he did not think that his experience of God in samadhi was genuine, because his face did not show it.

When he came to Sri Ramakrishna he saw he was in samadhi, and saw the wonderful radiance in his face. (That spiritual radiance finds expression through the face and physical frame in such a tangible way, that even the physical eyes cannot escape it.) Swami Shivananda said, "It was demonstrated before my eyes, and from that day I believed, really, that there is truth in samadhi, there is truth in God-realization, and God is real."

Sri Ramakrishna realized the absolute, impersonal Brahman. He realized the different aspects of Brahman — with form and without form — and knew that all these different disciplines lead to the same ultimate goal. His life was meant for the verification of the ancient spiritual teachings of Vedanta. Without the verification in life, spiritual ideals and practices have no meaning.

The scriptures say, "Love God with all your heart." Who loves God in this world with all his heart? Is it practical? Yes, it is practical. How do you know? See the life of Sri Ramakrishna, see the lives of the other great devotees of the Lord, and see if it is practical or not.

The scriptures say, "Live in this world with complete dependence upon God." Who depends on God? Everybody depends upon his bank balance, or something else — on children, or friends, etc. Is it practical? To see if it is practical, see the life of Sri Ramakrishna; see the lives of the other great spiritual leaders of the world. Spiritual teachings have no meaning, they cannot be a source of inspiration, unless you see them exemplified in the lives of the great ones.

In Vedanta principles and personalities go together. The principles are meaningless if they are not illustrated in the lives of great personages. Great personages are always, if they are great spiritually, the best exemplars of the spiritual truths. Where does devotion live? In the scriptures? If we squeeze the scriptures, will a drop of devotion come? A treatise on milk does not contain a single drop of milk. Similarly, a book on devotion, or a book on spiritual knowledge, does not contain a single drop of devotion or a single drop of knowledge. All great spiritual personages are more or less the verification of their own teachings. If we want to understand their teachings, we must understand them in the light of their lives.

In teaching Vedantic truths, the Ramakrishna Order finds the best illustration in the life of Sri Ramakrishna. Why? Because he is the most comprehensive exemplar of the Vedantic truths. In worshipping him, we worship Christ. We celebrate the nativity of Jesus Christ every year, read the Bible, and very often give discourses on Biblical topics. We do not think of ourselves as belonging to any particular religion, so general are our teachings, so universal; because we point to the basic truths which underlie all the religions of the world. We may not agree with all the dogmas of different religions, but we hold that the same fundamental truths are explicit, or implicit, in all the religions of the world.

We teach the Vedantic truths, the universal spiritual principles in the light of the life of Sri Ramakrishna. We do not actually preach Sri Ramakrishna. It does not matter whether a person worships Sri Ramakrishna as an Incarnation of God, or a messenger of God, or a prophet.

We believe Sri Ramakrishna to be the manifestation of Divinity, but we do not make it an article of faith; that is, we do not say that unless you accept Sri Ramakrishna as an Incarnation of God you cannot be accepted as a member of the Vedanta Society, or you cannot be accepted as a student of Vedanta. Who understands the sonship of God, who understands the human manifestation of the Divine Being? How does that Supreme Reality manifest Itself? "Incarnation" is just a mere word with most people. What does it matter that it is said that Sri Ramakrishna is an Incarnation of God?

Once a person came to Swami Shivananda and said, "Sir, is Sri Ramakrishna an Incarnation of God?"

Swami Shivananda said, "I still do not understand what an Incarnation means, I do not care to see that. I see his life, the best illustration of spiritual truths. God is real, He has many forms and aspects, and He can be realized in any of these aspects. There are many different ways to realize Him. The realization of Him is the highest goal of human life. Different religions lead to the same ultimate goal. These are the truths which Sri Ramakrishna has exemplified in his life. I look upon him as the very embodiment of the *Bhagavad Gita,* as the very embodiment of the *Upanishads,* as a mass of spirituality. I do not know whether he is an Incarnation, I do not know whether he is a prophet, or a messenger of God, or a son of God, or this or that — but here is the demonstration of spiritual truths. Whatever you call him, it does not make any difference. We do not care what designation you give to Sri Ramakrishna. We want you to understand his life."

Anyone who can bear the light of truth, who is not frightened by the light of truth, will understand Sri Ramakrishna's life. His life is one of the most shining examples in the spiritual history of mankind. There has never been such a complete demonstration of God-realization, such comprehensive manifestation of Divine Consciousness in any other human individual.

Sri Ramakrishna is associated with Vedanta not because this Order of Ramakrishna has its origin and source of inspiration in his life, but because he is the best exemplar of Vedanta. Without reading the Vedantic scriptures or the philosophical discussions contained in Vedantic literature, he realized God just through his appetite for God-realization. And from his experiences he stated the truths which tallied with the scriptures. Sri Ramakrishna's life verifies these scriptures.

It has been said in Vedantic literature that great spiritual personalities make the scriptures authoritative, because they verify the truths by their lives, by their experiences. Otherwise, what are the scriptures? Simply a mass of words. But the great spiritual personalities make the scriptures meaningful; they make life meaningful. This life is not just a playground of good and evil forces, it is not just an ever-changing mass of physical and psychical elements. All these physical and psychical elements are held together by spiritual reality shining within you as self-awareness. And that is the direct expression of Supreme Being. You can realize God just by realizing your very self. Sri Ramakrishna declared this truth.

It is said that Brahman is beyond words, beyond

thoughts. You cannot speak about *That*. It comes only through the highest realization. And so Sri Ramakrishna, in his own inimitable language, says, "Everything has been defiled, more or less, because it has been expressed by the human tongue; but Nirguna Brahman cannot be expressed, and so it is not defiled." Sri Ramakrishna simplified the most profound truths. My teacher used to say that we do not find a simpler exposition of the highest Vedantic truths than we find in the *Gospel of Sri Ramakrishna.*

There were other factors which make his life unique. For the first time in history a spiritual personage of great realization has been photographed. Also, his teachings have been recorded with stenographic accuracy. Mahendranath Gupta, who has recorded the *Gospel of Sri Ramakrishna,* used to keep a diary, and from that diary he wrote the *Gospel.* Teachings of previous renowned spiritual personages were not recorded directly as they were expressed. But in the case of Sri Ramakrishna they were directly reported. The facts in the lives of the great teachers are very meager. But in the life of Sri Ramakrishna the most common incidents are recorded. All the details are there.

Swami Vivekananda, who started the Vedanta movement, rarely spoke of Sri Ramakrishna. One hardly finds any reference throughout his writings and speeches. In the Western world where he lived for about three years, he spoke only once or twice of Sri Ramakrishna in New York — in remembrance of his birth anniversary. But Swami Vivekananda has given the truths that have been declared by the Vedantic scriptures, and these truths have been verified by Sri Ramakrishna.

The purpose of the Vedanta Society is not whether you worship Sri Ramakrishna or not, but that you become convinced of the highest spiritual truths, which Vedanta declares to be eternal and universal. In being convinced of these truths you come to know the meaning of life — that God can be realized; that is your goal.

Whatever way one thinks of Sri Ramakrishna, he is perhaps the most shining luminary in the spiritual history of the world, and we learn two great truths from his life — one, the realization of God is the ideal of life and can be attained in many different ways; and two, different religions are so many pathways to the realization of God. Basically there is no contradiction between one religion and another. These are the two great truths that stand out from the experience and teachings of Sri Ramakrishna, and merit constant repetition.

CHAPTER IV

HIS IMAGE: ITS SIGNIFICANCE*

Of the world's religious teachers of the highest order, Sri Ramakrishna was the first to be photographed. Today humanity has among its cherished treasures three different photographic portraits of the Divine Master, who is venerated by many as an Incarnation of God and by many more as a rare type of illumined soul. In carving the image of Sri Ramakrishna the distinguished artist, Malvina Hoffman, had the unique advantage of making his likeness true to life, inasmuch as she had not to depend solely on her imagination, past records, and hearsay, but was able to use photographs of the Master as her model.

None of his three photographs, however, portray Sri Ramakrishna on the plane of normal life, because each time he faced the camera he was absorbed in transcendental experience or mystical awareness (called in Sanskrit *samadhi*) while his countenance, radiant with superb joy, testified to the sublimity of his inner consciousness. Looking at one of his pictures Sri Ramakrishna once remarked, "It is a picture of a very exalted state of yoga. Time will come when this will be worshipped in many a home." Indeed, Sri Ramakrishna's portrait bears the impress of the state of

*The image referred to is the alabaster bust of Sri Ramakrishna which was unveiled at the Ramakrishna-Vivekananda Center, New York, on January 10, 1952.

God-consciousness and is therefore its veritable symbol. It is not possible to render in more realistic terms an expression of that ecstasy of Self-realization which thought cannot attain nor speech disclose.

The meditative poses of deities and of spiritual leaders such as Sri Krishna, Buddha, Shankara, and others delineated by Indian iconography are colored more or less by the conceptions of the artists. Sri Ramakrishna's whole personality was so suffused with divine love, purity, wisdom, and bliss that even in his lifetime he was recognized as the Supreme Spirit incarnate in human form. His image is therefore a genuine representation of the Divinity. I firmly believe that this sacred icon will help immensely in removing the veil of ignorance from the hearts of men and women and in revealing unto them the spiritual Reality it typifies.

Man feels the necessity of apprehending abstract ideas in concrete forms. It is the concrete expression that makes the abstract more vivid and real to him. So he has a tendency to represent the suprasensible in terms of the sensible. He also finds satisfaction in giving orderly expression to his conceptions, thoughts, and sentiments. Both these urges have been the creative force of fine art. It is the function of art to give concrete shape to the inner ideas and ideals. All genuine works of art are symbolic. As man learns mostly through the eyes and ears, he needs two distinct kinds of symbols: visible and audible. So art has two main forms of symbolic expression: architecture, sculpture, painting on the one hand, and music and poetry on the other.

Religion deals primarily with the suprasensible truths. So in the religious life of man there has been the imperative need of symbols, both visible and audible. In every religion there are symbolic presentations of spiritual truths. In its efforts to comprehend the Supreme Reality, to worship God with devotion and joy, to feel his presence vividly and intimately, the religious spirit of man has manifested itself in all kinds of art. But not all the fine arts have been prevalent in every religion. For instance, in Mohammedanism iconography and music seem to have no place. In Christianity dancing has not grown as an expression of religious sentiment. In Hinduism, however, all the avenues of art have been sought in approaching God. In the development of art, religion has played a distinctive role. Perhaps all the fine arts have their origin in religion.

Of the two main branches of iconography — sculpture and painting — the former has been prominent in Hinduism and Buddhism and the latter in Christianity. Both have deeply influenced the religious lives of people. Among the religious symbols the likenesses of God-men are particularly impressive and inspiring. The great spiritual leaders who are worshipped as divine Incarnations, messengers, or prophets, are the highest manifestations of God in human form. They make God real to us. We may conceive of God by speculative reason or by the study of books, yet we cannot be free from doubts as to His existence until we know the God-like personages. We can understand divine purity, divine love, divine power, divine wisdom, divine joy only through them. They represent God to us better than any celestial being. We cannot adore God but through them. Their images serve as natural symbols in the worship of the Divinity. They are most helpful to spiritual aspirants, especially at the early stage of development.

These God-men are the very embodiments of moral and spiritual principles. Their images signify the highest ideals. Worshipping God through such images is not idolatry. The great spiritual leaders are the best exemplars of their own teachings. Their lives demonstrate the truths they preach. The key to their message is in their own lives. We can comprehend the abstract principles only in the light of these personalities. Their human forms are the images of divine attributes.

It is the God-like personalities that implant on our minds the highest principles and truths as the very ideals of life. We may receive sublime ideas from various sources and ponder on them seriously; yet they will have no hold on us as ideals until we find them actualized in the lives of the great. It is our love and admiration for the great ones that sustains our moral and spiritual strength in the various trials and tribulations of life.

A person may be interested in religion, may study religious books, may speculate on God as assiduously as any research student of religion. He may even observe certain rites and forms, yet he may be lacking in the essentials of spiritual life. In order to be spiritual he should, in the first place, be convinced of the reality of God; secondly, he should understand that the realization of God is the supreme ideal of life; thirdly, he should find and follow the appropriate method of God-realization; and above all, he should have yearning for God. For all these requisites of spiritual life, particularly for the longing for God, which is the rarest of all, the aspirant needs inspiration from the great souls. Only the lovers of God can inspire us with the love of God.

The life of Sri Ramakrishna provides us with the most striking illustrations of these principles. He was born in an age when scepticism was the order of the day, when atheism and agnosticism were running rampant. He was immune to the spirit of the time. From his early age he missed God and God alone. His whole being was crying for the direct experience of God. He turned his back completely upon the sensible world and plunged into the struggle for God-realization. He practiced, one after another, not only the multifarious courses of Hinduism, but also the methods of Mohammedanism and Christianity. He realized God through each one of them.

Experience of God differs according to the nature of the spiritual discipline. Sri Ramakrishna's realization covers the entire range of spiritual experience given to man. He had the transcendental experience of the impersonal absolute Brahman. He was aware of God's presence in the universe as the all-pervasive supreme principle. He saw God dwelling in the hearts of all as their innermost Self. He also attained his complete unity with the Divinity through every relationship of love. He was so well established in the realm of the spirit that his mind went up and down the whole gamut of supraconscious experience with perfect ease.

Indeed, Sri Ramakrishna's life is a complete demonstration of the fact of God-realization. Here he stands supreme. The world has been sorely in need of such evidence. From direct experience he declared:

God is real.

He has many aspects and forms.

He can be realized.

The ways of realization differ according to the capacities and tendencies of individuals.

The different religions of the world are so many pathways to God realization.

The realization of God is the supreme ideal of life.

He also prescribed the service of God in man as the universal spiritual discipline.

The reality of God, the realization of God, the harmony of religions, and the service of God in man are the four cardinal points of his message. It centers on the teaching that the supreme object of human life is the realization of God. Man should live with this end in view. Nothing else can be an end in itself. It is the goal not only of his religious but also of his worldly activities. All the life values, material, intellectual, aesthetic, and moral must subserve the spiritual ideal. Social, political and economic systems should be built so as to facilitate the spiritual growth of man. Thus there will be harmony in all the aspects and activities of life. The ultimate goal is one and the same but the ways vary according to individuals' psychophysical and environmental conditions. All men and women, at whatever levels of life they may be, can reach the Goal through progressive courses. Even from the bottom of a pit a man can direct his steps towards the mountain-top.

Let one and all live in this world as pilgrims to the shrine of Truth. This is the secret of world unity, peace and progress. The supreme ideal is indispensable to both the spiritual and the material growth of man. Whenever worldly greatness and glory become the primary objectives of life, man's moral nature and intellect degenerate, being subordinate to them. How can there be peace and progress in such a case? So Sri Ramakrishna's message furnishes the key to man's spiritual development and material well-being in individual and collective life.

The image of Sri Ramakrishna is a deeply significant and inspiring emblem of spirituality.

CHAPTER V

THE CLASSIFIED TEACHINGS
OF SRI RAMAKRISHNA

(Extracts from his daily conversations as recorded by "M," an intimate disciple.)

A. *To realize God is the goal of human life. This is immortality and blessedness unlimited.*

The goal of life is the attainment of God. Work is only a preliminary step, it can never be the end. Even unselfish work is only a means, it is not the end.

Devote yourself to spiritual practice and go forward. Through practice you will advance more and more on the path of God.

Now dive deep into the Ocean of God. There is no fear of death from plunging into this Ocean, for this is the Ocean of Immortality.

I said to Narendra, "Look here, my boy. God is the Ocean of Bliss. Don't you want to plunge into this Ocean? Suppose there is a cup of syrup and you are a fly. Where will you sit to sip the syrup?" Narendra said, "I will sit on the edge of the cup and stick my head out to drink it." "Why?" said I. "Why should you sit on the edge?" He replied, "If I go far into the syrup, I shall be drowned and lose my life." Then I said to him: "But my child, there is no such fear in the Ocean of Satchidananda [Being-Consciousness-Bliss]. It is the Ocean of Immortality. By plunging into It a man does not die, he becomes immortal. Man does not lose his mind by being mad about God."

B. *After realizing God the illumined one can live with pure love for Him and see Him in all things and beings.*

At first one discriminates, "Not this, not this," and feels God alone is real and all else illusory. Afterwards the same person finds that it is God Himself who has become all this — the universe, maya, and the living beings.

First of all reach the indivisible Satchidananda [Being-Consciousness-Bliss] and then, coming down, look at the universe. You will then find that everything is His manifestation. It is God alone who has become everything. The world by no means exists apart from Him.

There are three classes of devotees. The lowest one says, "God is up there." That is, he points to heaven. The mediocre devotee says that God dwells in the heart as the "Inner Controller." But the highest devotee says, "God alone has become everything."

All that we perceive is so many forms of God. It is God Himself who plays about as human beings. If God can be worshipped through a clay image, then why not through a man?

All doubts disappear when one sees God. It is one thing to hear of God, but quite a different thing to see Him.

A man should reach the Nitya, the Absolute, by following the trail of the Lila, the Relative. It is like reaching the roof by the stairs. After realizing the Absolute, he should climb down to the Relative and live on that plane in the company of devotees, charging his mind with the love of God. This is my final and most mature opinion.

C. *Self-effort is necessary for the purification of the heart.*

A man must work. Only then can he see God. One day in an exalted mood I had a vision of the Haldarpukur [a pond in his native village, Kamarpukur]. I saw a low-caste villager drawing water after pushing aside the green scum. Now and then he took up the water in the palm of his hand and examined it. In that vision it was revealed to me that the water cannot be seen without pushing aside the green scum that covers it; that is to say, one cannot develop love of God or obtain His vision without work. Work means meditation, japa, and the like. The chanting of God's name and glories is work too. You may also include charity, sacrifice, and so on.

If you want butter, you must let the milk turn to curd. It must be left in a quiet place. When the milk becomes curd, you must work hard to churn it. Only then can you get butter from the milk.

How much of the scriptures can you read? What will you gain by mere reasoning? Try to realize God before anything else. Have faith in the guru's words, and work. If you have no guru, then pray to God with a longing heart. He will let you know what He is like.

It will not do to say that God exists and then idle away your time. You must reach God somehow or other. Call on Him in solitude and pray to Him, "O Lord! reveal Thyself to me." Weep for Him with a longing heart. You roam about in search of "woman and gold" like a madman; now be a little mad for God. Let people say, "This man has lost his mind for God." Why not renounce everything for a few days and call on God in solitude.

What will you achieve by simply saying that God exists and doing nothing about it? There are big fish in the Haldarpukur, but can you catch them by merely sitting idly on the bank? Prepare some spiced bait and throw it into the lake. Then the fish will come from the deep water and you will see ripples. That will make you happy. Perhaps a fish will jump with a splash and you will get a glimpse of it. Then you will be so glad!

A man wanted to see the king. The king lived in the inner court of the palace, beyond seven gates. No sooner did the man pass the first gate then he exclaimed, "Oh, where is the king?" But there were seven gates, and he had to pass them one after another before he could see the king.

The vision of God depends on His grace. Still a man must work a little with longing for God in his heart. If he has longing he will receive the grace of God.

Let me tell you something. God can be seen. The Vedas say that God is beyond mind and speech. The meaning of this is that God is unknown to the mind attached to worldly objects. Vaishnavcharan used to say, "God is known by the mind and intellect that are pure." Therefore it is necessary to seek the company of holy men, practice prayer, and listen to the instruction of the guru. These purify the mind. Then one sees God. Dirt can be removed from water by a purifying agent. Then one sees one's reflection in it. One cannot see one's face in a mirror if the mirror is covered with dirt.

D. *With the purification of the heart one receives the grace of God.*

After the purification of the heart one obtains divine love. Then one sees God, through His grace.

One cannot see God without purity of heart. Through attachment to "woman and gold" the mind has become stained — covered with dirt, as it were. A magnet cannot attract a needle if the needle is covered with mud. Wash away the mud and the magnet will draw it. Likewise, the dirt of the mind can be washed away with the tears of our eyes. This stain is removed if one sheds tears of repentance and says, "Oh God, I shall never again do such a thing." Thereupon God, who is like the magnet, draws to Himself the mind, which is like the needle. Then the devotee goes into samadhi and obtains the vision of God.

You may try thousands of times, but nothing can be achieved without God's grace. One cannot see God without His grace. Is it an easy thing to receive the grace of God? One must altogether renounce egotism, one cannot see God as long as one feels, "I am the doer." Suppose, in a family, a man has taken charge of the storeroom. Then if someone asks the master, "Sir, will you yourself kindly give me something from the storeroom?" the master says to him, "There is already someone in the storeroom. What can I do there?"

God doesn't easily appear in the heart of a man who feels himself to be his own master. But God can be seen the moment His grace descends. He is the Sun of Knowledge. One single ray of His has illumined the world with the light of knowledge. That is how we are able to see one another and acquire varied knowledge. One can see God only if He turns His light toward His own face.

The police sergeant goes his rounds in the dark of night with a lantern in his hand. No one sees his face, but with the help of that light the sergeant sees everybody's face, and others, too, can see one another. If you want to see the sergeant, however, you must pray to him, "Sir, please turn the light on your own face. Let me see you." In the same way one must pray to God, "O Lord, be gracious and turn the light of knowledge on Thyself, that I may see Thy face."

E. *Devote yourself to spiritual practice until the goal is reached.*

Repeat God's name and sing His glories, keep holy company, and now and then visit God's devotees and holy men. The mind cannot dwell on God if it is immersed day and night in worldliness, in worldly duties and responsibilities. It is most necessary to go into solitude now and then and think of God. To fix the mind on God is very difficult, in the beginning, unless one practices meditation in solitude. When a tree is young it should be fenced all around, otherwise it may be destroyed by cattle.

To meditate you should withdraw within yourself or retire to a secluded corner or to the forest. And you should always discriminate between the real and the unreal. God alone is real, the Eternal Substance. All else is unreal, that is, impermanent. By discriminating thus, one should shake off impermanent objects from the mind.

Do all your duties, but keep your mind on God. Live with all — with wife and children, father and mother — and serve them. Treat them as if they were very dear to you, but know in your heart of hearts that they do not belong to you.

Cry to the Lord with an intensely yearning heart and you will certainly see Him. People shed a whole jug of tears for wife and children. They swim in tears for money, but who weeps for God? Cry to Him with a real cry.

God reveals Himself to a devotee who feels drawn to Him by the combined force of these three attractions: the attraction of worldly possessions to the worldly man, the child's attraction for its mother, and the husband's attraction for the chaste wife. If one feels drawn to Him by the combined force of these three attractions, then through it one can attain Him.

The point is, to love God even as the mother loves her child, the chaste wife her husband, and the worldly man his wealth. Add together these three forces of love, these three powers of attraction, and give it all to God. Then you will certainly see Him.

F. *The path of devotion is not as difficult to follow as the path of knowledge.*

But you should remember that the heart of the devotee is the abode of God. He dwells, no doubt, in all beings, but He especially manifests Himself in the heart of the devotee. A landlord may at one time or another visit all parts of his estate, but people say he is generally to be found in a particular drawing-room. The heart of the devotee is the drawing-room of God.

He who is called Brahman by the jnanis [seekers of the knowledge of Impersonal Absolute Being] is known as Atman [Indwelling Self] by the yogis and as Bhagavan [God of love and grace] by the bhaktas [devotees]. The same brahmin is called priest, when worshipping in the temple, and cook, when preparing a meal in the kitchen. The jnani, sticking to the path of knowledge, always reasons about the Reality, saying, "Not this, not this." Brahman is neither "this" nor "that;" it is neither the universe nor its living beings. Reasoning in this way, the mind becomes steady. Then it disappears and the aspirant goes into samadhi. This is the Knowledge of Brahman. It is the unwavering conviction of the jnani that Brahman alone is real and the world illusory. All these names and forms are illusory, like a dream. What Brahman is cannot be described. One cannot even say that Brahman is a Person. This is the opinion of the jnanis, the followers of Vedanta [non-dualistic] philosophy.

But the bhaktas [devotees] accept all the states of consciousness. They take the waking state to be real also. They do not think the world to be illusory, like a dream. They say that the universe is a manifestation of God's power and glory. God has created all these — sky, stars, moon, sun, mountains, ocean, men, animals. They constitute His glory. He is within us, in our hearts. Again, He is outside. The most advanced devotees say that He Himself has become all this — the twenty-four cosmic principles, the universe, and all living beings. The devotee of God wants to eat sugar, not to become sugar.

The Saguna Brahman [Supreme Being with attributes]

is meant for the bhaktas. In other words, a bhakta believes that God has attributes and reveals Himself to men as a Person, assuming forms. It is He who listens to our prayers. The prayers that you utter are directed to Him alone. You are bhaktas, not jnanis or Vedantists [non-dualists]. It does not matter whether you accept God with form or not. It is enough to feel that God is a Person who listens to our prayers, who creates, preserves, and destroys the universe [dissolves into the causal state], and who is endowed with infinite power.

It is easier to attain God by following the path of devotion.

G. *God is both Personal and Impersonal. He has forms and attributes. He is also beyond them both.*

Some say that God has form and is not formless. Thus they start quarrelling. A Vaishnava [worshipper of Vishnu, Personal God] quarrels with a Vedantist [seeker of Impersonal Brahman].

One can rightly speak of God only after one has seen Him. He who has seen God knows really and truly that God has form and that He is formless as well. He has many other aspects that cannot be described.

Well, what suits your taste — God with form or the formless Reality? But to tell you the truth, He who is formless is also endowed with form. To His bhaktas He reveals Himself as having a form. It is like a great ocean, an infinite expanse of water, without any trace of shore. Here and there some of the water has been frozen. Intense cold has turned it into ice. Just so, under the cooling influence, so to speak, of the bhakta's love, the Infinite appears to take a form. Again, the ice melts when the sun rises; it becomes water as before. Just so, one who follows the path of knowledge — the path of discrimination — does not see the form of God any more. To him everything is formless. The ice melts into formless water with the rise of the Sun of Knowledge. But mark this: form and formlessness belong to one and the same Reality.

H. *One and the same God is called by different names. All religions lead to Him. One can reach Him by any of them if one sincerely seeks Him.*

It is not good to feel that one's own religion alone is true and all others are false. God is one only, and not two. Different people call on Him by different names: some as Allah, some as God, and others as Krishna, Shiva, and Brahman. It is like the water in a lake. Some drink it at one place and call it "jal," others at another place call it "pani," and still others at a third place and call it "water." The Hindus call it "jal," the Christians "water," and the Moslems "pani." But it is one and the same thing. Opinions are but paths. Each religion is only a path leading to God, as rivers come from different directions and ultimately become one in the one ocean.

The Truth established in the Vedas, the Puranas, and the Tantras is but one Satchidananda. In the Vedas It is called Brahman, in the Puranas It is called Krishna, Rama, and so on, and in the Tantras It is called Shiva. The one

Satchidananda is called Brahman, Krishna, and Shiva.

With sincerity and earnestness one can realize God through all religions. The Vaishnavas will realize God, and so will the Shaktas, the Vedantists, and the Brahmos. The Moslems and Christians will realize Him too. All will certainly realize God if they are earnest and sincere.

Some people indulge in quarrels, saying, "One cannot attain anything unless one worships our Krishna," or "Nothing can be gained without the worship of Kali, our Divine Mother," or "One cannot be saved without accepting the Christian religion." This is pure dogmatism. The dogmatist says, "My religion alone is true and the religions of others are false." This is a wrong attitude; God can be reached by different paths.

CHAPTER VI

LIFE AND TEACHINGS OF SRI RAMAKRISHNA IN THE MODERN AGE

One can very well wonder what significance the life of Sri Ramakrishna can possibly have in this modern age. His life to all appearance was unlike that of a modern man. A modern man is well dressed; Sri Ramakrishna was not at all well clad; he was not even half-clad, I may say. He does not even look like a modern man.

A modern man is for acquisition; Sri Ramakrishna preached renunciation. He preached renunciation of that to which the modern man clings desperately — woman and gold. Think of it! By 'woman' he did not mean actually 'woman' but lust. He meant that women should not be looked upon simply as objects of pleasure. They should be worshipped, not with the spirit of gallantry, but as the very image of the Divine Mother. It is in this sense, he said, that one should renounce his attachment to women.

Modern man clings desperately to the sense-bound world. Sri Ramakrishna turned his back completely on the sense-world and plunged into the unseen in order to realize that Ultimate Reality. A modern man aims to live on as much as possible, and Sri Ramakrishna aimed to live on as little as possible. He lived an antiquated life.*

But in one respect Sri Ramakrishna was ultra-modern — in his approach to God. There he was more modern than

*See Appendix C. "Sri Ramakrishna's Message of Renunciation and Realization in terms of Vedanta."

any modern man. We generally depend — if we ever care for the knowledge of God — upon scriptural study, or on philosophical reasoning. But Sri Ramakrishna did not depend on either of these ways, because neither of these ways, scriptural texts nor inference based on experience, can conclusively prove the reality of God. It is the consensus of most philosophers that one cannot know God simply through reasoning. Reasoning is inherently incapable of either proving or disproving God conclusively. And scriptural texts claim to be revealed words, but they do not reveal God to us.

So Sri Ramakrishna asked, "What is the proof of existence?" The answer was, it is direct perception, and it is the primary source of knowledge upon which all other means of knowledge are established. With this scientific attitude, he thought, "If God is real, if the Divine Mother symbolized by this image is real, I must see that." And he actually realized God. Not by one particular method, not in one particular aspect; but he finished almost all the important spiritual lessons of the world in the course of twelve years.

In this age of materialism, scepticism, and agnosticism, Sri Ramakrishna's life is meant to demonstrate fundamental spiritual truths by actual experience. That was the mission of his life.

What are these fundamental spiritual truths? From direct experience he declared that God is real. The reality underlying this manifold is God, who is the very perfection of existence. *The Real is the Ideal.* This imperfect universe has perfection as its very basis and being. Self-luminous, pure consciousness is the reality underlying each and every transitory form. That is his declaration, and this message has served to re-orient human knowledge. It is a challenge to all those ideas, all those theories that declare that the ultimate reality is simply blind, material substance; or that the ultimate reality is just blind energy, or some kind of vital principle bereft of consciousness, or some kind of blind will. Sri Ramakrishna says, "No!" Each and every form of existence presupposes consciousness. That which is self-existent must be self-luminous. That which is self-luminous must be self-existent. The ultimate reality can be only absolute consciousness.

This absolute consciousness, the ultimate reality, must be recognized by all branches of knowledge. Any branch of knowledge which is contradictory to this fundamental truth cannot be accepted as faultless. It may be a psychological truth, it may be scientific truth, it may be a philosophical truth — any theory that antagonizes this fundamental reality cannot be accepted as true.

Then again he says, "God can be realized." There have been great philosophers like Herbert Spencer who said God is unknown and unknowable; even Kantian philosophy ends in a kind of agnosticism. Sri Ramakrishna says, "No!" It is true that the fundamental reality is perfection itself, but that can be realized. That fundamental reality actually shines in the heart of each and every individual as the innermost self. By realizing the self you realize the Self of the universe. God can be realized — from direct experience. And this God-realization is the ideal of human life, and also serves as a great regulating principle in modern life.

What is the ultimate goal of human life? Is human life destined to seek security in the insecure? Does this drama of birth, growth, decay and death mean the whole of life? Has man no other ideal to pursue than to run after transitory pleasures and possessions? Sri Ramakrishna says, "No!" The ultimate goal of life is the attainment of the highest ideal, and the highest ideal is God. Your highest ideal is God. You cannot conceive of anything higher than that.

In this age, when human minds desperately cling to the sense-bound universe, Sri Ramakrishna says, "No!" This innermost longing in your heart for complete freedom, for unalloyed joy, for unmixed blessing, for eternal life, *can* be fully satisfied — you can realize God. The realization of God is immortality itself, beatitude unlimited, and you can reach that. You are potentially *that* and because of that you are constantly seeking higher and higher life. The theory that man is moving toward perfection, of which there is no end, means that man is potentially perfect. This evolution becomes meaningless if you say material existence alone is the root of life. If this life is rooted in matter, how can it flower into spiritual consciousness? If something base is your origin, you cannot develop into something pure and blessed. The fundamental reality is perfection itself. That is your origin, and to go back to that origin is your goal.

It is this declaration which has made this life meaningful; that is, Sri Ramakrishna turns the human mind from growing secularism to spiritual idealism. He makes modern life meaningful. Not only that, spiritual idealism is indispensable to the security and soundness of our material existence. Man's material welfare depends very much on his moral well-being. If this moral life is not sound, material well-being can never be sound. At the back of all political and social problems is the lack of inner integrity of individuals and nations. By declaring spiritual idealism to be the highest goal, Sri Ramakrishna not only makes this life meaningful, but also makes this material existence, this progress of life, secure and sound, because the only secure foundation of moral life is the spiritual unity of human souls. A person can never be unselfish in the true sense, a person cannot develop what we call all-embracing love, a man cannot really perform a disinterested act in the true sense, if he cannot feel a spiritual relationship with his fellow-beings. Without spiritual idealism human morality cannot be secure.

Our moral life depends very much upon the ideal we follow, the ideal we seek. If our ideal of life is to be happy and prosperous in this sense-plane, naturally our knowledge, our philosophy, our ethics, our aesthetics, will be subservient to this. There is a persistent desire in man to be happy and prosperous. He asks himself — "What is knowledge good for, what is the scientific attitude good for, what is ethics good for, if they cannot enable me to live prosperously, gloriously, happily in this life?" Naturally all human branches of knowledge, ethics, aesthetics, etc., in this case will be subservient to material existence, subservient to man's greed; and when all these different aspects of cultural life become subservient to human greed, naturally they deteriorate. When moral life deteriorates, it cannot sustain the other aspects of life any more.

So the spiritual idealism of Sri Ramakrishna has made

this life meaningful, and also has provided a secure basis for this life.

Sri Ramakrishna said, from his own experience, that God can be realized not just by one particular method; but God can be realized in many different aspects and forms, and He can be realized in His formless, featureless aspect. A person can approach God according to his capacities, tendencies and conditions of life. Sri Ramakrishna declared that the different religions of the world are actually so many paths to reach the highest, and this message the world needed. Fanaticism and bigotry have covered the world with religious feuds; torn asunder human beings, and communities.

Sri Ramakrishna emphasized there should be harmony of religions, there should be unity of all religions. This unity is a great desideratum in this age. Never have human beings felt the need of unity among themselves as they have felt at this time, because the different parts of the world have been knit closely together by marvelous scientific achievements in transportation and communication, and human beings have come to realize that they have to rise or fall as a whole. Mankind has to rise or fall as a whole. The interest of any section of humanity is indissolubly woven with the interests of others, and if religions cannot settle their differences — religion which avowedly stands for peace and unity — how can you expect unity in other fields of life?

Sri Ramakrishna's message has tended to a great extent to broaden the religious ideas of the modern time. Bigotry is disappearing. Almost all the religions now recognize the truth in other religions as well; and since the advent of Sri

Ramakrishna there has been the beginning of the decline of materialism. Human minds are veering to spiritual idealism. There has been a spiritual rebirth since the end of the nineteenth century, unperceived though it may be.

Sri Ramakrishna declares further from his own experience that a person can live in this world after God-realization. He can actually see God in all things and beings, an all-pervading, self-luminous reality. He says those who live on this relative plane after coming down from the plane of the absolute, have true devotion. They actually develop love for all, because they realize their essential unity with the supreme reality that exists in all creatures as the indwelling self. They really feel love for all. He encouraged his disciples to seek this devotion, this knowledge — that is, that after realizing the absolute, the impersonal One, a person should come down and live in this world in full consciousness of the Divinity for the guidance of humanity. Only rare individuals are capable of this, however. Very few can realize God before the term of life is over. If a person does realize God, his life usually ends with that experience. Rare individuals realize God, and even after God-realization live in this world. Hindu scriptures recognize this truth.

We find in the *Bhagavatam,* "Such are the blessed qualities of the Divine Lord, that seers who realize God as the absolute, impersonal being, who find supreme satisfaction in the realization of one all-pervading Self — they also live in this relative existence, offering their heart's devotion to the Lord in His personal aspect." It has always been recognized in Vedanta that a person can actually live in this body after realizing the highest. But in actual practice this has not been emphasized. The emphasis of orthodox schools has always been on realizing God. Whether or not you would then live in this world — for the guidance of humanity with all-embracing love — was not their main concern. This truth is there, though there was not much of its actual practice. Sri Ramakrishna emphasized this point.

Swami Turiyananda (Hari) came to Sri Ramakrishna one morning. Sri Ramakrishna asked him, "Well, Hari, what do you want?"

"Moksha,"* he forthwith replied.

"You are small-minded," Sri Ramakrishna rejoined.

The Swami looked at him in wonderment and thought within himself, do not all Vedanta books proclaim moksha to be the highest goal of life?

"You see," continued the Master, "the expert chess players are so sure of winning the game that they deliberately turn down the pieces before reaching the goal in order to continue the play."

We find that Swami Vivekananda after realizing the impersonal, absolute being, attaining *nirvikalpa samadhi,* came to Sri Ramakrishna. Sri Ramakrishna said, "Now you have the experience."

"Yes."

"What do you want?"

"I want to be completely immersed in bliss, in absolute silence and blessedness."

"No, this is not for you; you have to fulfill the Divine Mother's great mission for which you have come, and until

*Union with God or knowledge of the ultimate Reality, moksha is a human being's final liberation from all bondages of worldly life.

you finish that, the key will be with me."

And Swami Vivekananda, though he had a continuous tendency to be merged in the Absolute, held his individuality in this relative plane and had all-embracing love. With that attitude he lived in this world. He started a mighty organization for the regeneration of India, and for the reconstruction of humanity upon a spiritual foundation, thus fulfilling one great mission of Sri Ramakrishna's life.

Another contribution of Sri Ramakrishna in the modern age is his teaching that if man can worship God through symbols or images, he can worship God in human form. One day somebody referred to the teaching of a Hindu spiritual leader, saying that he emphasized compassion. Sri Ramakrishna said, "Why compassion? It means condescension. Who are you to be compassionate to the children of the Lord! Not compassion, but serving your fellow-beings in the spirit of serving God." It is the temple of the body where God actually shines.

This is the message that Swami Vivekananda at once took up. And on the basis of this message he organized the Ramakrishna Math and Mission.

He emphasized not only the realization of God, but also working for humanity as a spiritual discipline, trying to see God in all. The great seers see God, but when spiritual aspirants try to see God — the ideal becomes the practice; they are not inherently different. Practice means the partial realization of the ideal and always means a graded way to the goal, however high it may be. Practice does not mean that you are here and the goal is always there. No, you are climbing the steps through practice; it forms the graded way to the highest goal. A person who can continue this practice persistently should never be discouraged. If you follow any kind of discipline for gaining some talent or power, you know that with practice you are proceeding towards the goal.

That goal which the great seers reach becomes a method of practice for the spiritual aspirants. The spiritual aspirant with effort tries to think of the Lord in all and to cultivate the love which comes from that vision. Swami Vivekananda wanted particularly that in this age human beings become convinced more than ever of their latent possibilities, and come to know that they are potential seekers of God — or in other language, that they are the very divinities of the Lord on earth. This attitude, according to Sri Ramakrishna and Swami Vivekananda, should reshape human relationships and man's dealings with his fellow beings.

Should we not make any distinction between man and man? Yes, we should, because there are differences in the psychophysical systems. But while noticing differences we should not forget the potential divinity of each and every person. If a person commits a crime he can be punished, but without bitterness. You should recognize that right within this criminal dwells the free Divine Being, covered with some dross and dirt for the time being. So Sri Ramakrishna said, "Recognize this." A mother punishes the child, but the mother's heart is never embittered, there is always love; the mother knows this is her child. Here is the brother, or here is the child of the Lord, and for the time being his potential divinity is covered and through ignorance he has indulged in something wrong which has to be rectified. Due punishment can be administered, without any bitterness, if a person always holds in his consciousness the understanding that the same Supreme Being dwells in all individuals as the innermost self.

The spiritual truths realized by Sri Ramakrishna that have a great bearing on modern life and thought can be summarized as follows:

1. God is real — the very basis of this imperfect world is perfection itself, self-luminous reality; no theory should be antagonistic to this, the basic reality.

2. God can be realized. He is not just an unknown and unknowable entity, but He can be realized, and this realization is the goal of life.

3. This longing for eternal life, for absolute peace and blessedness can be completely fulfilled.

4. There are many ways to the attainment of this goal.

You are not destined to hold to this material existence till the end of life — your real goal is realization of God, and the attainment of complete self-fulfillment. There are many ways to reach this. This spiritual idealism makes your entire life secure.

Any scheme of life without spiritual idealism is incomplete — take it for granted. Sri Ramakrishna says unequivocally that the goal of human life is the realization of God. One can be very far away from the goal; one can stand at the bottom of a very low pit, but by directing his steps gradually, he can reach the highest. Swami Vivekananda has given the message that each individual has to reach the highest ideal, God, *from where he is* along his own line of development. Each religion is a pathway to the same Supreme Being variously conceived. Even through secularism one will move toward spiritual idealism. You do not have to give up everything, but at whatever level of life you may be, you can gradually direct your steps towards the highest.

In this age Sri Ramakrishna declared that a person can live in this world after God-realization. It is then and then alone that a person can see God everywhere, can have true all-embracing love, and can do real good to humanity because he knows the ultimate goal of life. He himself would say, "I see the same Narayana, the same Indwelling Being in all."

We should try to see the Divinity dwelling in all, and help all to manifest their divinity. In helping others to manifest their divinity, we manifest our own divinity. All relations with our fellow-beings should be with this inner attitude of seeing God in ourselves and in others. The whole world will then be blessed. There will be unity, peace, and happiness and prosperity if humanity holds to these spiritual truths.

Part II

THE AUTHOR'S REMINISCENCES OF
HOLY MOTHER AND SOME DIRECT DISCIPLES
OF SRI RAMAKRISHNA*

*Of the sixteen Apostles of Sri Ramakrishna — Swami Vivekananda, Swami Brahmananda, Swami Premananda, Swami Saradananda, Swami Shivananda, Swami Abhedananda, Swami Turiyananda, Swami Akhandananda, Swami Subodhananda, Swami Vijnanananda, Swami Yogananda, Swami Niranjananda, Swami Ramakrishnananda, Swami Adbhutananda, Swami Advaitananda and Swami Trigunatitananda — the author has had the privilege of seeing Swami Vivekananda, and meeting the remainder of the first ten.

CHAPTER VII

REMINISCENCES OF SRI SARADA DEVI, THE HOLY MOTHER, AND GLIMPSES OF HER INBORN MOTHERLINESS

When I went to Calcutta for the first time in January-February, 1908, I planned to see Holy Mother after seeing Master Mahasaya, but for some reason or other my objective was not achieved. Perhaps Holy Mother was not in Calcutta at the time; she had been living at Jayrambati, her birth-place.

It was during my second visit to Calcutta in December, 1911, that I had the blessed privilege of seeing Holy Mother. I went to the Udbodhan Office building at Baghbazar one Wednesday afternoon by streetcar from the locality where I stayed. Holy Mother's living quarters were upstairs. Through the covered main entrance I entered the small courtyard. There I met a monk in ochre cloth, whom I had known at Dacca. He was Kapil Maharaj, as far as I remember his name. I told him that I had come to see Holy Mother.

He told me that outside devotees were allowed to see Holy Mother only on Tuesdays and Saturdays. I said, "I have come to Calcutta on a short visit. I cannot stay till Saturday." Then he told a young sadhu, who had access to Holy Mother's room, to inform her that a young devotee from Dacca had come to see her and that he would not be able to stay in Calcutta until the next Saturday. With Holy

Mother's permission the young sadhu escorted me to Holy
Mother's room upstairs.

At one end of the room was a shrine as it is at present.
At the other end in one corner there was a flat wooden cot on
which was Holy Mother's bedding. Holy Mother used to sit
on the cot with her feet on the floor. As I entered the room I
noticed that some women devotees, who had been seated on
the floor at Holy Mother's feet, left the room and went into
the adjoining room.

Holy Mother had her usual veil over her head. I bowed
down to Holy Mother and took the dust of her feet. I said
that I had come from Dacca and implored her blessings. She
raised her right hand indicating her blessings and spoke a
few words. Just then the same young sadhu appeared at the
door and waved his hand indicating that I should go to him.
As I went out of the door to the verandah he gave me some
offered fruits and sandesh in a leaf cup. I ate the prasad,
washed my hands, and was going back to the room when the
sadhu said to me, "No, today your visit is over."

It was mainly during the summer vacation that I went
to Calcutta and Belur Math. Holy Mother generally lived at
that time at Jayrambati. She returned to Calcutta usually
after the worship of the Divine Mother, Jagaddhatri, in
October-November. I had been told that Kamarpukur and
Jayrambati were malarial places. Having lived in the city all
my life I was not encouraged to go there, especially in the
rainy season.

It was in the summer of 1915, as far as I can remember,
that Swami Premananda told me to take with me a picture
of Holy Mother and worship it. He also wrote a note to

Rasbehari Maharaj (Swami Arupananda) at the Udbodhan Office instructing him to give me a picture of Holy Mother. I went to Rasbehari Maharaj with the note and got the picture from him. It may be mentioned here that as long as Holy Mother was alive her pictures were not for sale. I held the picture as a treasure and returned to Dacca with it.

I installed the picture close to the picture of Sri Ramakrishna in my shrine at Mohini Babu's house, where I had lived since 1905 and conducted the work of the Ramakrishna Association.

Since my first visit to the Maharaj (Swami Brahmananda) on Thursday, February 6, 1908, I had gradually become more and more drawn to him. I clearly remember this day because it happened to be the day of the worship of the Goddess Saraswati, the bestower of knowledge. The Maharaj treated me very affectionately from the very first meeting. During all my visits I tried to keep close to him as much as possible.

It was in January, 1916, that the Maharaj came to Dacca via Mymensingh after visiting the Holy Temple of Kamakhya near Gauhati. He was accompanied by Swami Premananda, Swami Shankarananda, Swami Madhavananda, and other senior and junior sadhus. I remember the names of most of them. There were no less than twelve in the party, including a devotee (Bibhuti Babu). The party was accommodated in a stately building (Agnes Villa) belonging to a landlord who usually lived in the country. For the time being the house was unoccupied. During the Maharaj's stay there I would see him once or twice daily. Every day a number of visitors, including some men and women of distinction, used to come and pay respects to the Swamis. Many college and school students were also among the visitors.

At Dacca the Maharaj was graciously willing to give initiation to some devotees (men and women). One afternoon I approached him for spiritual instruction. He said, "You come and see me at Belur Math."

The next summer (1916) I went to Belur Math. As soon as I found an opportunity I approached the Maharaj for initiation. The Maharaj said, "Wait, wait. I have to see the almanac and find an auspicious day. It is not easy to give initiation." In this way a few days passed.

Meanwhile a small party of young devotees, mostly newcomers, were getting ready to go to Jayrambati to receive initiation from Holy Mother. The party included Prabhu (Maharaj), later Swami Vireswarananda, the present President of the Ramakrishna Math and Mission. On seeing them my mind deviated. I thought it was a unique opportunity to accompany them to Jayrambati and receive initiation from Holy Mother. In a few days all were ready for the trip. Along with them I bowed down to the Maharaj and took leave of him. We covered a part of the way to Jayrambati by train. Then we all traveled on foot along a vast meadow. Altogether there were six or seven in the party.

Late in the afternoon I had dysentery. It developed into blood dysentery, because of which I had to halt repeatedly. My companions told me to rent a bullock cart. I got into the cart and lay down inside. The cart moved on almost all night. One of the party Saradindu (Maharaj), later Swami

Viswanathananda, who was my close friend for many years, was following the cart. Because of my ailment I had to stop the cart off and on. The rest of the party were walking ahead and behind not far from us.

Early the next day we came to a river not far from Jayrambati. On the way Saradindu (Maharaj) repeatedly told me that in my ailing condition I should not go to Holy Mother, because my sickness would embarrass her extremely. So he urged me to return to Calcutta. He further said that it would be proper for me to approach the Maharaj again for initiation. I was quite reluctant to turn back. At the same time I was very apprehensive of causing the least trouble to Holy Mother. I finally decided to return. I ordered the cart-driver to turn back. Of his own accord Saradindu (Maharaj) accompanied me.

The next day we returned to Calcutta. Meanwhile my condition had improved. I went to a relative in Calcutta. He welcomed me and took every possible care of me. Within a few days I regained my normal health.

Then I went to Belur Math. Meanwhile the story of my turning back had reached the Math and many of the devotees came to know about it. After bowing down to the shrine I bowed down to Swami Premananda. "You cannot achieve your object until the time is ripe," he remarked. Next I went to see the Maharaj. I was very much afraid of meeting him. I thought he would scold me. On seeing me he simply uttered a Sanskrit saying meaning "Many are the obstacles to the spiritual Goal." He treated me tenderly and said nothing more. I felt very much relieved.

Still there was wavering in my mind as regards asking

him for initiation. I had the feeling that Holy Mother was greater than the Maharaj. So I thought I should try to go to her again and receive initiation. Next afternoon as Swami Shivananda (Mahapurush Maharaj) was strolling up and down near the embankment on the Ganges at Belur Math, I approached him with these words, "Maharaj, some take initiation from Holy Mother, some from the Maharaj. Is there any difference?"

Mahapurush Maharaj, who was always very kind to me, said, "No, I see no difference. You get the same Ganges water from two different faucets. The same grace of Thakur descends through Holy Mother and through the Maharaj. But what do you mean by 'some *take* initiation.' No, they *get* it, they *get* it. It is *given,* it is *given.*" As I heard these words my inner attitude was transformed. I thought, "Who am I to *take* initiation. I have to see from whom I get it."

At once I went back to the Maharaj and implored him again for initiation. The Maharaj said the same thing: "Wait, I have to see the almanac and find an auspicious day. It is not easy to give initiation. I have to work hard." A few days later I approached him again. He gave me preliminary instruction and told me to see him next time when he would return from his trip in Southern India.

After receiving the instruction I went back to Dacca and wholeheartedly followed the course. Holy Mother returned to Calcutta toward the end of the summer in 1916. Swami Premananda graciously sent me a card in his own handwriting informing me of her presence in Calcutta. But being preoccupied with the Maharaj's instruction I did not make any effort to make the trip to Calcutta to see Holy

Mother.

The Maharaj came back to Calcutta in the autumn of 1917. On receiving the news I went to Calcutta and visited the Maharaj. He was gracious to give me initiation about a month later. During this period Holy Mother was not in Calcutta. Later my situation in life did not permit me to have the privilege of being in Holy Mother's presence a second time. She entered into Mahasamadhi in July, 1920.

However, I had the privilege of being present at the dedication ceremony of Holy Mother's temple on her birth-place at Jayrambati in April, 1923, inaugurated by Swami Saradananda, on which occasion more than one hundred sadhus of our order and many more devotees from Calcutta and other places assembled. The festival continued a number of days. Thousands of villagers from far and near were sumptuously fed. It was one of the most impressive functions I have witnessed in my life. I also had the opportunity of visiting Kamarkupur and other adjoining places associated with the life of Sri Ramakrishna and of Holy Mother.

Referring to Holy Mother, Swami Premananda once remarked: "There is one who even beat [defeated] Sri Ramakrishna."

This reminds me particularly of the following two incidents in the life of Holy Mother:

(1) A queer woman who looked upon Sri Ramakrishna as her beloved was a cause of annoyance to many. Not only the disciples but even Sri Ramakrishna tried to avoid her. But Holy Mother always welcomed her, consoled her, and

encouraged her to come to her when others turned her away. One day Sri Ramakrishna expressed his disapproval of her indulgence. At this Holy Mother answered, "Pardon me. If I turn her away, where will she go? It is impossible for me to refuse her shelter and solace when she comes to me."

(2) At Dakshineswar it was the daily practice of Holy Mother to carry Sri Ramakrishna's supper from her scanty living quarters to his room, which was about sixty feet away. One evening as she was proceeding with the plate of food in her hands, a woman, who often visited the place, came forward and said, "May I carry it, mother?" With these words she took the plate from Holy Mother's hands, brought it to Sri Ramakrishna, and left. Then he turned to Holy Mother and said, "How can I eat this food? It is defiled. Why did you allow her to carry it? Do you not know that she is an impure woman?" "Yes, I know that," said Holy Mother and implored him to eat the food. "All right," said Sri Ramakrishna, "But you promise that this will never happen again and that none but you will bring my meal." "Yes, I myself will continue to bring the food," said she, "But I cannot be promise-bound. In case someone comes to me, calls me mother, and asks for the privilege of carrying the food to you, I cannot refuse. You are the Master of all, and not of me alone."

Indeed, Holy Mother was a mother by nature. As an ideal wife she loved Sri Ramakrishna and as an ideal disciple she adored him. Silently and patiently she served him, disregarding all physical discomforts, from day to day for years, with full attention and affection. Indeed, her whole life was characterized by self-denying service, a distinctive mark of motherhood. Her motherly affection permeated her wifely duties to Sri Ramakrishna, which she performed with meticulous care.

What a life of self-imposed spiritual discipline she lived while serving Sri Ramakrishna at Dakshineswar! She used to get up at 3 o'clock in the morning and sit in meditation. Often she became deeply absorbed in it. On moonlit nights she would look at the moon and pray with folded hands, "May my heart be as pure as the rays of yonder moon!" Or, "O Lord, there is a stain even in the moon, but let there not be the least trace of stain in my mind!"

I have heard from Yogin Ma[1] in Benares (1921) that Holy Mother used to say the same prayer at Radharamanji's temple in Vrindavan, where she went shortly after Sri Ramakrishna's Mahasamadhi. Yogin Ma had already been there in Vrindavan.

A vivid account of Holy Mother's self-denying service to Sri Ramakrishna is given by Swami Saradananda:

[1]A disciple of Sri Ramakrishna, and a companion and attendant on Holy Mother for many years. She lived a unique life of austere habits and devotional practices. Swami Saradananda used to take care of her as well as of Holy Mother. It was after the passing of Holy Mother (July, 1920) that Yogin Ma went to Benares with Swami Saradananda before Maharaj's arrival there in January, 1921. In Benares we noticed her daily practice of hard austerities and devotional rites. She outlived Holy Mother about three years.

Another daily companion and attendant on Holy Mother was Golap Ma. She lived with Holy Mother at Udbodhan House and dedicated herself to the service of Holy Mother and to household duties. An interesting episode of Sri Ramakrishna's visit to Golap Ma's house on July 28, 1885, can be found in the *Gospel of Sri Ramakrishna.*

Although she was staying in the Nahabat[1] in the north of the garden at Dakshineswar and engaged herself daily in the service of the Master, no one else, except two or three boy devotees[2] whom the Master himself introduced to her, ever saw her holy feet or heard her words during that long period. Although she lived the whole day in that small room and prepared varieties of food twice daily for the Master and the devotees, no one could know that anyone was engaged in doing those duties there. She left her bed every day a little after three in the morning, long before anyone else rose from sleep and having performed the personal duties of the morning including ablutions in the Ganga, she entered that room and never came out during the whole day. Calmly and silently she finished all her work with wonderful quickness and engaged herself in worship, japa and meditation.[3]

She rendered the same self-denying service to Sri Ramakrishna in the rented house at Shyampukur in Calcutta, where he was taken for medical treatment. To quote Swami Saradananda:

As soon as she heard that the Master's illness might increase if he was not provided with diet prepared in strict accordance with the instruction of the doctor, the Holy Mother came to the Shyampukur house without the least hesitation and gladly took charge of preparing the diet without at all considering her own convenience in staying there. One is simply surprised at the

[1]The concert tower at the northwest corner of the temple ground. Holy Mother used to live in a tiny octagonal room on the ground floor, all around which there was a verandah about four feet wide. The floor area of Holy Mother's room was approximately 50 sq. ft. There was a corresponding concert tower in the southwest corner of the temple ground. Concerts were held on the upper stories of both the towers at the time of the worship during the lifetime of Rani Rasmani.

[2]Latu (Swami Adbhutananda), Yogen (Swami Yogananda) and also aged Gopal Senior (Swami Advaitananda).

[3]*Sri Ramakrishna, The Great Master,* pp. 840-41.

thought that she underwent all kinds of physical inconvenience and did her duty, staying in a house of one apartment only for three months among unknown men.

Although there was only one place for all to take bath in, etc., no one knew when she finished all these things in the morning and went up to the terrace near the steps leading to the roof of the second floor before 3 a.m. She spent the whole day there, prepared diet, etc., for the Master at proper times and then sent word downstairs through Swami Adbhutananda or the old Swami Advaitananda. At that time people were asked to move away and she brought the diet downstairs and fed the Master or we ourselves brought it down, according to convenience. At midday she took her food and rested there. At 11 p.m. when all were asleep, she came down from that place and slept till two in the morning in the room in the first floor allotted to her. Fortifying her heart with the hope of the Master's recovery, she spent day after day in that way. She stayed there so silently and unobservedly that even many of those who visited the house every day could not know that she lived there and took upon herself the hardest and most important job in the service of the Master.[1]

Obviously her motherly nature prevailed in her self-denying service to Sri Ramakrishna. She had motherly love for all. Anyone, pure or impure, high or low, wise or unwise, could claim her as mother. Her all-embracing love overcame all social barriers and religious conventions.

At Jayrambati, her native village, she not only cooked for her disciples, of whatever caste, but even removed their plates and washed their dishes after they had finished their meals. The guru was ministering to the disciples, while it was the duty of the disciples to minister to the guru! It was unthinkable that she, who was adored as the very image of

[1] *Sri Ramakrishna, The Great Master,* p. 844.

the Divine Mother, who held in her hands the key to salvation, who belonged to the topmost Brahman caste, should do menial service to the lowliest of her disciples! Naturally they protested. But she silenced them all, saying in an affectionate yet firm voice, "Am I not your mother?" Though there were some women devotees to do the household work, she liked to do most of it herself.

Another outstanding instance of her motherly love for one and all is cited below.

Not far from Jayrambati there was a small settlement of Mohammedan peasants. They used to cultivate silkworms for a living. They lost this means of livelihood because of the failure of the silk industry due to competition in foreign trade. Many of them became day-laborers and even committed robbery at night to augment their slender income. They became notorious all around as night prowlers. Then a famine broke out in that area. With the approval of Holy Mother Swami Saradananda decided to build a cottage for her at Jayrambati. Many of these Mohammedan laborers were engaged in the work. The villagers were frightened in the beginning, but later they remarked that even the robbers had turned devotees through the grace of Holy Mother.

One day Holy Mother wanted to feed a Mohammedan laborer. He was given a seat in the verandah of her room in the inner section of the house. Her niece, Nalini, was serving food. Holy Mother noticed that the girl was dropping food on his plate from a safe distance for fear of being contaminated. She at once came forward and said, "How can he enjoy the food if you serve in this manner? Let me serve." After the man had eaten Holy Mother herself removed his plate and cleaned the place. At this Nalini, her niece, protested: "You should not do this, dear aunt, you will be an outcast." Holy Mother rebuked her and said, "Just as Sarat [Swami Saradananda] is my son, so is Amzad [the Mohammedan laborer]."

Holy Mother's life testifies to the fact that motherhood does not consist just in the capacity for child-bearing, but in that spirit of service which joyously undergoes all privations and sufferings for the sake of the beloved. The mother's lips cannot utter a single word of curse on the child under the gravest provocation. It is said in a Sanskrit verse that there can be a bad child but no bad mother. Every woman is a potential mother. Her motherly nature usually develops with the bearing of a child. She may develop it even without bearing a child.

After Holy Mother's marriage her mother once remarked, "My Sarada is married to an eccentric. She will never hear the sweet address 'mother,' 'mother.' " When this was reported to Sri Ramakrishna, he remarked, "Wait! Time will come when she will be tired of being addressed as 'mother,' 'mother.' "

CHAPTER VIII

REMINISCENCES OF SWAMI VIVEKANANDA

I had the privilege of seeing Swami Vivekananda three days, in March, 1901, when he visited Dacca, the chief city of East Bengal. I was then a school boy.

About a year before Swami Vivekananda came to Dacca an American lady, Madame Marie Louise of New York, who had accepted the Hindu religion and philosophy and had been initiated into monastic life as Swami Abhayananda, visited the city. It was early in April, 1900, as far as I remember. She had been accommodated in a mansion-like house in our neighborhood.

The house belonged to a premier zemindar (landlord) of East Bengal (Mohini Mohan Das, usually called Mohini Babu), who had passed away several years ago without leaving any issue. He was a widower, though his aged mother was still living. From time to time she occupied an inner section of the house with her maidservants and cook. In the front part of the house on the ground floor there lived a gatekeeper and a caretaker, and there was also an office for the management of the estate.

The owner's nephew Jatindra Mohan Das (nicknamed Jatin Babu), a sister's son, was in charge of the house and happened to be interested in the teachings of Sri Ramakrishna and his disciples. It was Jatin Babu who had invited the American lady when she had been at Belur Math on a visit, and he arranged for her accommodation in

Mohini Babu's house. I was curious to know why the house had been decorated at the time. A cousin of mine, who was my senior in age and for whose opinion I had some regard, said to me, "Do you not know that an American lady who has become a Hindu has been staying in the house?" "What!" I said. "An American lady has become a Hindu! How could it happen? She must be an enlightened woman."

In those days we considered America to be in the forefront of the civilized world. "Do you not know that Swami Vivekananda," added my cousin, "went to America and made the Americans Hindus?" "Americans have become Hindus!" I said. "Then Swami Vivekananda must be a god. Is not Hinduism a bundle of superstitions!" This was the impression we got in those days from Christian missionaries (generally Hindu and Moslem converts) who used to preach from crowded street corners.

I immediately decided to go and see her. I entered the house and found her seated on a chair on the ground floor in the second courtyard. I was looking at her closely and trying to find marks of Hinduism on her. She was grayhaired and dressed in a long white gown and wore socks and slippers. I did not notice any sign of Hinduism except a rosary of rudraksha beads around her neck.

This was the time of an annual Hindu festival welcoming the new year. Musical parties came with singing and dancing to amuse her. She was an elderly lady and was smiling as she watched the parties of singers and dancers holding torches in their hands. It was evening time. When I returned home I came to know that a party of women of the neighborhood had gone to see her out of curiosity. They came back with the report that she had become a veritable Hindu, because she was a vegetarian and observed fast on the eleventh day of the lunar fortnight like an orthodox Hindu. When I heard this I had no more doubt that she had become a Hindu.

Shortly after this I went back to my cousin and inquired of him about Swami Vivekananda. He told me that Swami Vivekananda was a disciple of Sri Ramakrishna Paramahamsa, who had lived at Dakshineswar near Calcutta. He added that Keshab Chandra Sen, the third great leader of the Brahmo Samaj, a socio-religious reform movement of modern India, was a great admirer of Ramakrishna Paramahamsa, who had convinced him of the significance of image worship. At that time Keshab Chandra Sen had won the hearts of many by his eloquence and devotional fervour. On hearing my cousin, my heart was filled with great admiration for both Swami Vivekananda and Sri Ramakrishna.

It so happened that about a year later toward the end of March, 1901, the same house had again been decorated. A huge arch of welcome with flags and festoons had been raised across the street. My curiosity was aroused. Upon inquiry I was surprised to know that Swami Vivekananda was coming the same day in the afternoon. Some leading citizens of Dacca, members of the reception committee, had already gone to the adjacent railroad station to accord him a hearty welcome on behalf of the citizens. I lost no time in reaching the gate of the house anxiously waiting for the Swamiji's arrival.

At last Swami Vivekananda came in a magnificent

open landau carriage drawn by a pair of horses. The carriage stopped at the gate. I stood very close to the door of the carriage and was watching Swami Vivekananda. He got down escorted by two prominent attorneys of the city who had accompanied him from the railroad station. I looked at the Swamiji closely. He noticed me. I was the only young boy there. I do not remember whether I bowed down to his feet or not. He had an ochre turban on his head, and wore the usual monastic shirt. He was heavily garlanded with marigold flowers.

The Swami was escorted across the front yard and the porch to the first floor, where arrangements had been made for his residence. Very soon a large crowd of citizens, who had been to the railway station to welcome the Swami, gathered in the front yard and the porch and crowded the stairway leading to the first floor. These were all grown up people; I was young. I did not want to stay there any longer.

The next day after school hours I walked down to that house in expectation of seeing Swami Vivekananda. He came down from the first floor escorted by a group of men and college students. He had put on a long ochre robe reaching down close to his ankles. He had the usual monk's cap on his head; in his hand he carried a walking stick. He was followed by a large crowd as he walked across the street to the riverside, for the purpose of taking a walk on the paved road along the embankment of the River Budiganga. On the other side of the long road there was a park. I followed the crowd for a while and then came back.

The following day I was disappointed in not finding Swami Vivekananda. I was told upon inquiry that he had gone down the river in a houseboat to a distant place of pilgrimage called Langal-bundh, on the river Brahmaputra, for the purpose of an immersion in the river on an annual festival day. Thousands of Hindu pilgrims used to gather there every year from far and near for the sacred bath (Varunisnan). Some of his monastic disciples who had accompanied Swamiji on his trip from Calcutta also followed him there on the occasion. His mother with a few close relatives arrived there from Calcutta with his approval for the purpose of the pilgrimage. All came to Dacca on the Swamiji's return.

During his absence I would inquire every afternoon after school hours whether the Swami had returned. One afternoon I was told that he had come back from his trip to Langal-bundh and was staying in the houseboat on the river. As I ran down to the riverside, I noticed Swami Vivekananda inside the houseboat. He was all by himself. On either side of the boat there were rows of large windows. He was pacing back and forth in the drawing room of the houseboat with his arms folded across his chest as in the Chicago posture. He was bare-headed and his face was not clean-shaven at the time. He had put on an ochre-colored dhoti and an undershirt (similar to what the young people here wear and call "t"-shirts).

I walked down close to the boat and looked at him through the windows from outside. When Swami Vivekananda saw me he sat down on a long bench attached just below the rows of windows on the side close to the bank. He looked at me through one of the windows while resting his arm on the window sill. There were a few boys who stood behind me at a distance. Very soon a party of gentlemen came. They went inside the boat. Swami Vivekananda received them cordially. A conversation started as they were seated. Then I left the place.

Thus I saw Swami Vivekananda three days. During his stay at Dacca he met parties of visitors at least twice a day and talked with them. He also gave two public lectures, which were well-attended. I was too young to attend the lectures. The impression left on me by Swami Vivekananda has been a source of inspiration all my life. I can still visualize him as I saw him. Later I secured and read whatever literature regarding him I could obtain, in English or in Bengali.

With a few disciples and his mother's party, Swami Vivekananda left Dacca for pilgrimages to Chandranath near Chattagram (East Bengal) and Kamakhya near Gauhati in Assam. From Gauhati he went to Shilong, a hill station and the capitol of Assam. There he was cordially received by Sir Henry Cotton, Chief Commissioner of Assam.

About two years before his visit to Dacca Swami Vivekananda had sent two of his disciples, Swami Virajananda and Swami Prakashananda, for the propagation of the message of Sri Ramakrishna in East Bengal. They lived in the same Mohini Babu's house as the guests of Jatin Babu. A religious association was formed and weekly meetings were started. But the two Swamis did not stay long. This religious association published *A Short Account of the Life and Teachings of Swami Vivekananda* after his passing away. I was much impressed by this booklet.

For many years this same house was the center of the
Ramakrishna Movement at Dacca and was visited at
different times by Swami Saradananda, Swami Premananda, and Swami Brahmananda. It was from this center that
the permanent site of the Ramakrishna Math and Mission at
Dacca was secured in 1915. Early in 1916 Swami
Brahmananda laid the foundation stone of the
Ramakrishna Math, and Swami Premananda laid the
foundation stone of the Ramakrishna Mission there.

It may not be out of place to mention in this context
that from the autumn of 1905 I had the privilege of carrying
on the work of the Ramakrishna Association with the
cooperation of Jatin Babu, who lived in his own house with
his family. The main function of the Association was the
holding of a weekly meeting every Saturday evening
throughout the year. After the reading of the *Gospel of Sri
Ramakrishna,* a discussion was held and devotional songs,
usually in chorus, were sung by different religious parties.
The birthday festivals of Swami Vivekananda and Sri
Ramakrishna were celebrated enthusiastically each year and
were attended by large crowds.

A few years later a philanthropic body was organized,
mainly with college students, to help the needy and the
distressed in whatever way possible. I used two rooms on the
second floor (with separate entrance and stairway), the one
as my study and bedroom and the other as a shrine. The
meetings of the Association were held in an adjoining hall. I
had my meals in my uncle's home where my widowed
mother lived. The activities of the Association continued the
same way until a full-fledged Ramakrishna Math and

Mission was established on the new site with monastic members early in 1917. About the same time the Saturday meetings and the lending library were shifted to another house close to the previous one.

CHAPTER IX

REMINISCENCES OF MASTER MAHASAYA ("M")

It was at the end of January, 1908, that I had the first opportunity to leave my home city, Dacca, at that time the capital of the Province of East Bengal and Assam, for a trip to Calcutta, which was then the capital of British India and of West Bengal. I was a first year student of an Intermediate college located in Dacca and affiliated with the University of Calcutta. I came to Calcutta, accompanied by a relative with a concession travelling ticket of about ten days, mainly for the purpose of pilgrimages.

While Dacca is situated on the river Budiganga, Calcutta is situated on the Ganges, which derives from the Bhagirathi, the main stream of the Ganges (Ganga). According to Hindu astrology there was to be a rare auspicious day for a sacred bath in the Ganges on account of the solar eclipse at early dawn. The auspicious day happened to be, as far as I can recall, on Monday, February 3. The day was further sanctified by the special position of a notable constellation. Most probably I arrived in Calcutta on the previous Saturday, February 1.

Being closely connected with the Ramakrishna movement at Dacca from an early age, I had been familiar with the names of most personages and places associated with the life of Sri Ramakrishna, and within the reach of Calcutta. I had the good fortune to see Swami Vivekananda three days when he visited Dacca in March, 1901. I also had the privilege of carrying on the work of the Ramakrishna Association at Dacca since the autumn of 1905. We used to read *The Gospel of Sri Ramakrishna* (the *Kathamrita*) in our weekly meetings held every Saturday evening. Then there were devotional songs.

On my arrival in Calcutta I naturally felt an urge to meet "M," Master Mahasaya, the author of *The Gospel of Sri Ramakrishna,* who lived in the city not far from the place where I stayed. It was early evening (probably Saturday, February 1) that I went by streetcar to his parental home at Gurudas Chowdhury Lane close to Amherst Street. As I entered the house I inquired about Master Mahasaya. I was told to walk up to the fourth floor on the brick built stairway in front of the building.

As I reached the fourth floor I found Master Mahasaya seated with a group of devotees inside a porch before the attic, which was used as the shrine. Surprisingly I saw a close friend of mine, nicknamed Sagar Babu, reading *The Gospel* before the group. I noticed Master Mahasaya was very attentively listening to the reading of *The Gospel of Sri Ramakrishna* (the *Kathamrita*). I was surprised. I thought to myself, "How strange, he who has written *The Gospel* has been listening to its reading like a pupil!"

I was very happy to see my friend Sagar Babu there, who had come from Dacca to Calcutta to study medical science. After the reading was over there was a short discussion and then the devotees left except Sagar Babu, who greeted me and introduced me to Master Mahasaya as a close friend of his who was intimately connected with the Ramakrishna Association at Dacca.

After he, too, had left Master Mahasaya talked with me and inquired about the Ramakrishna Association at Dacca. Then he told me to go inside the shrine and take out the small (metallic) glass of offered water and a sandesh offered on a small (metallic) plate. As directed by him I went outside the porch and drank the offered water and ate the offered sandesh.

As I was going to sit before Master Mahasaya within the porch, he inquired, "Where did you put the plate? Where is the glass?" I told him that I had left them outside the porch. "No, no," he said. "This will not do. You should·wash them." Then I walked down the stairs to the ground floor, where there was a faucet of water. With quick steps I returned. Master Mahasaya told me to dry the glass and the plate and keep both in proper places, in proper order. He told me at the same time that Thakur was very orderly and neat and clean. He used to put things in such a way that one could find them at night even in darkness. (It is to be noted that in those days there were no electric lights.)

Then Master Mahasaya made further inquiries about me and our activities at Dacca. I said, "We are trying to establish an ashrama at Dacca on the outskirts of the city. Our friend, Sagar Babu, who has married into a very wealthy family, has granted us several acres of land for this purpose. We have already started a center there with a hut, and one of our young associates who wants to be a monk has been living there."

I further said to Master Mahasaya that our plan was to establish temples there of different religions in accordance with Thakur's teaching of the harmony of religions. With great enthusiasm I described that there would be on the same site a Hindu mandir (temple), a Mohammedan mosque, a Christian church, and a Buddhist temple. I added that gradually there would be temples of other religions, and that there would be an appropriate sign on each of the temples. Further, at the gate of the monastery a big signboard "The Temple of Harmony of Religions" would be fixed. I spoke with youthful enthusiasm and Master Mahasaya listened quietly.

As I stopped, Master Mahasaya spoke out:

"This is what you want, signboard and advertisement; self-advertisement. This is not Thakur's idea. According to Thakur one should gather something here within the heart [pointing his finger to his heart] before he launches on public work. First of all you should have devotion to God. Until you have that you are nowhere. You are simply *frittering* your energies, *frittering* your energies. Thakur said, again and again, that one should pray to God in solitude and secrecy (nirjane gopane)."

"Nirjane gopane," he repeated several times. He then quoted a parallel passage from the Bible: "But thou, when thou prayest, enter into thy closet and when thou hast shut thy door, pray to thy Father, which is in secret; and thy Father, which seeth in secret shall reward thee openly." (St. Matthew 6:6) I kept quiet; I could not say a single word anymore.

Then Master Mahasaya said to me, "Since you have come to Calcutta for the first time you should see the Holy Mother, the Maharaj, and Baburam Maharaj; you must visit Belur Math and Dakshineswar." I already had planned to visit these holy places and bow down to the holy personages.

I had to return to Dacca in about a week. Each time I had an occasion to go to Calcutta I made it a point to see Master Mahasaya and bow down to him. But this was the first and last time that Master Mahasaya scolded me. After that he always received me cordially and often treated me with two rasagollas (juicy balls) offered to Sri Ramakrishna. From the second time on I usually met him on the fourth floor of the Morton Institute on Amherst Street, of which he was the proprietor and Headmaster. Once I met him at Belur Math. I do not remember the details of each visit but he invariably talked about Sri Ramakrishna.

It was in December, 1911, that I visited Calcutta the second time, when I was a fifth year graduate college student. I came to Calcutta on a concession ticket with a group of my classmates, on the occasion of the visit of Emperor George V of England.

I took the earliest opportunity to see Master Mahasaya. I walked up to the fourth floor of the Morton Institute to meet him. He was at that time all by himself. In the course of conversation I said that Thakur used to see the Divine Mother. Master Mahasaya gravely told me, "No, not *seeing* only! The Divine Mother *talked* with him and he used to talk with the Divine Mother, just as we are talking!"

On several occasions I found him reading one or another Vedanta book. On my arrival he would pass the book to me, asking me to read some of the pages. After the reading was over he talked a little while on the topic and then on Sri Ramakrishna. His purpose was to avoid vain talk.

One day I found him reading *Yogavasistha Ramayanam* (Bengali tr.). As I came to see him he wanted me to read a few pages of the book.

One other occasion I remember as well as the first one. It was in the year 1924 in early winter on my return from pilgrimages in the Himalayas and several holy places in Northwestern India. From Hardwar I went to Vadarika Ashrama on the Alakananda, and the temple of Kedarnath on the Mandakini. On my return I lived about a month at Hardwar on the Ganges, and the next month in our Sevashrama (Home of Service) at Kankhal. Then after a short stay at our Kishenpur Ashrama, a retreat for monks near Dehradun, I went on a pilgrimage to Amarnath in Kashmir with a party of four monastic brothers.

On my way back to Calcutta I visited a number of holy places in Kashmir, the Punjab, and the Northwestern province. I felt a special urge to visit Naimisaranya, where Suta Goswami had related the *Srimad Bhagavatam* before an audience of sixty thousand, including many saints and sages. The main story of the *Srimad Bhagavatam* was narrated originally by Suka Deva (a born-free soul), to King Parikshit on the eve of his leaving the body; Suta Goswami was present then among the audience.

From Lucknow I came to the small railroad station Balamo. From Balamo I walked up to Naimisaranya. I saw there the extensive meadow where the audience of sixty thousand had gathered. In one part of this meadow there were a few water tanks and temples.

On my way back I visited a few other places including Benares, and then came down to Calcutta. When I went to see Master Mahasaya, he inquired about my pilgrimages. He showed particular interest in Naimisaranya, and asked me how I went there and what kind of place it was. Then he remarked, "Ah, so many holy places you have seen! Had Thakur seen you, he would have gone into samadhi; but I do not get into samadhi!"

From this time on I lived a number of years at Dacca Ashrama, Mayavati Ashrama, and the Delhi center. Whenever I happened to be in Calcutta I invariably saw Master Mahasaya. During most of my visits I met one or more of the three devoted pupils of Master Mahasaya, Gadadhar, Binaya, and Jagadbandhu.

Master Mahasaya had deep regard for the monastic ideal. Since he came to know my decision to enter into monastic life he would never allow me to touch his feet when I bowed down to him. He spoke very highly of the true monks. In his opinion a householder and a monk both can be highly advanced in spiritual life, still there will be a difference between the two as between two ripe mangoes (or apples) of two different grades.

The last time I saw Master Mahasaya was in the summer of 1931, when Mahapurushji Maharaj (Swami Shivananda) sent me back to Delhi to take charge of the work there. On the eve of my departure for Delhi, one evening I came to Morton Institute on Amherst Street and wanted to see Master Mahasaya. Someone escorted me to his bedroom with his permission. He was ill in bed. When he came to know about my going to Delhi, he greeted me as I bowed down to him. He passed away on the 4th of June, 1932.

CHAPTER X

REMINISCENCES OF SWAMI BRAHMANANDA

It was on Thursday, February 6, 1908, the day of the worship of the Goddess Saraswati, the bestower of knowledge, that I had the blessed privilege of seeing Maharaj (Swami Brahmananda) for the first time. Having been closely associated with the ideals and activities of the Ramakrishna Order from my early age, I was looking for the earliest opportunity to visit Dakshineswar, the Belur Math, and bow down to such personages as the Holy Mother, Swami Brahmananda, and Master Mahasaya, the recorder of *The Gospel of Sri Ramakrishna.*

It was on the occasion of a pilgrimage for immersion in the Ganges on a rare auspicious day, that I came to Calcutta with a relative of mine on a ten day railway concession ticket. I was then a first year college student of an Intermediate college located at Dacca and affiliated with the University of Calcutta. The auspicious day happened to be Monday, February 3, particularly because of the solar eclipse at early dawn.

On the following Thursday afternoon I was able to arrange for a trip to the Belur Math. I got onto a ferry boat at Baghbazar, which dropped me at a landing ghat across the river to the south of the original gate of the Belur Math. On entering the Belur Math I saw at the southwestern corner of the Math ground a one-story building built to the memory of Girish Chandra Ghosh. To the north of that building on the bank of the Ganges there was the incomplete memorial of Swami Vivekananda built a little higher than the ground level. The statue of Swami Vivekananda, carved from a marble slab, was installed there.

As I was walking over the extensive grassy lawn toward the original Math building, I noticed from a distance that Maharaj (Swami Brahmananda) was seated on the open porch to the south of the Math building with his feet resting on the step to the porch. He was wearing slippers. I was overjoyed that on entering the Belur Math for the first time the first person I saw was the Maharaj. I would have considered this a mere coincidence had I not been told in later years that Swami Prabhavananda and Swami Akhilananda had somewhat similar experiences.

At the time Maharaj was watching the cows that were grazing in the meadow beyond the fence to the south of the Math building. Evidently he was resting after strolling on the grassy lawn for a while. I had seen Maharaj's photograph a number of times so I could easily recognize him. As I bowed down and touched Maharaj's feet he blessed me. Standing before him I said that I had come from Dacca. Then he asked me where I lived at Dacca. I said, "I live in the same Mohini Babu's house where Swamiji stayed."

It may be mentioned here that I had the blessed privilege of seeing Swami Vivekananda three days toward the end of March, 1901. From the autumn of 1905 I used to live in that very house and make necessary arrangements for the weekly meeting of the Ramakrishna Association, held every Saturday evening for the study of the *Gospel of Sri*

Ramakrishna, discussion on related topics, and devotional songs usually in chorus.

I thought Maharaj had also accompanied Swamiji to Dacca because with Swamiji there were several senior Swamis. Naturally I assumed Maharaj was acquainted with the locality. I was going to describe to him the location of the house where my mother lived with my uncles and where I used to have my meals. On hearing this Maharaj said, "No, no, I did not go with Swamiji." "You did not go to Dacca with Swamiji!" I said. "Will you take me?" said Maharaj. I said, "Yes." Then he said, "How?" I said, "I know Jatin Babu who invited Swamiji and was his host. He is a very good friend of ours and is generous. I will tell him and he will make all arrangements for your going to Dacca." Maharaj smiled, "Oh, this is how you will take me!" Maharaj then made inquiries about some of the devotees of Dacca whom he knew. Then he told me to go to the shrine and also meet Swami Premananda.

I went to the shrine upstairs on the north side of the courtyard at the back of the original building. Downstairs were the kitchen, the dining place, and stores. As I came down the steps from the shrine I was given some offered fruits and sweets in a leaf cup. I went to the Ganges to wash my hands. As I came up the landing steps I saw an elderly venerable Swami walking down. I bowed down at his feet and asked, "Where is Swami Premananda?" He then pointed to his chest saying, "Here, why?" Then I bowed down to his feet again, and said "Maharaj has told me to see you."

Then I went back to Maharaj to take leave of him

because I intended to go to Dakshineswar that afternoon. Maharaj told me how to go to the nearest ferry-ghat to the north of the Math, and asked a junior monk to show me the back door. I went to the ferry-ghat, waited for some time but no boat was available. Then I went to the next ferry-ghat further north and then to a third. By that time it was dark.

Fortunately I met a gentleman with whom I was able to cross the river by ferry-boat. He told me that because of the Saraswati puja the boatmen had worked all day, so they got tired and went home earlier. He also advised me not to venture to go to Dakshineswar in darkness. He even invited me to pass the night in his house, but I decided to come back that very night to my relative with whom I lived in order to save him worry. Not even a share-carriage was available. I had to walk all the way to Calcutta where my relative lived. I fell sick and decided to return to Dacca before the term of the concession ticket was over.

It was in December, 1911, that I saw the Maharaj the second time. I was then a fifth year student at Dacca College affiliated with the University of Calcutta. I came with some of my classmates on the occasion of the visit of the British Emperor of India, George V. It is to be noted that Calcutta was then the capital of the Province of Bengal and of the Indian Empire of Britain. I stayed in a relative's house in Calcutta.

Before coming to Belur Math this time I had visited Dakshineswar, and also had seen Holy Mother at Udbodhan House. After coming to Belur Math I first went to the shrine and had some prasad and was looking for Maharaj. I found him seated on a big bench on the ground floor of the verandah of the monastery building, facing the Ganges. From the very first visit I felt much drawn to Maharaj. I bowed down to him, took the dust of his feet and sat on a narrow bench in front of him.

It was about 11 o'clock in the morning when an elderly gentleman arrived. As soon as he entered the porch Maharaj got up and bowed down to his feet. I was wondering who this gentleman might be. He had come all the way wearing slippers. Maharaj looked at me and said, "Do you know who he is?" I said, "I saw him worshipping the Divine Mother at Dakshineswar." "Yes, you are right, he is our Ramlal Dada, Thakur's nephew," said Maharaj. Then I understood why Maharaj promptly left his seat and bowed down to the newcomer's feet.

After a while Maharaj took Ramlal Dada to the dining hall for the midday meal. I also had prasad along with other sadhus and devotees sitting on the adjoining porch. I met Maharaj again before leaving the monastery. He said to me, "You should come here as often as you can. You will not be the loser." Although I had been closely associated with the Ramakrishna Order from my early age and I had great admiration for monastic life, I did not know that I could ever be a monk. His remark assured me of my prospect of being a monk.

Although I had visited the Belur Math a few times since February, 1908, I did not spend the night there. It was during the summer vacation in 1915 that I came to live there for the first time. I was in close touch with Swami Premananda, the abbot of the monastery, throughout the vacation, but did not see Maharaj, who was then staying at

Bhadrak (District Balasore, Orissa) in Balaram Bose's estate building.

The third time I met the Maharaj was early in January, 1916. It was at Dacca. The Maharaj visited the place accompanied by Swami Premananda and a number of senior and junior sadhus. There were twelve altogether in the party, including a devotee of good standing. The Maharaj and his party came to Dacca after visiting the temple of the Divine Mother Kamakashi at Kamakhya near Gauhati. In the temple of the Divine Mother Maharaj performed a special worship.

On the way to Dacca the party stayed a few days in Mymensingh at the invitation of the devotees there. The Maharaj and his party arrived at Dacca at night by railway train, which was unduly late. I was waiting at the railway station with a landau carriage drawn by two horses, which belonged to a friend of mine.

I escorted Swami Brahmananda and Swami Premananda to Agnes Villa, a stately building, where arrangements were made for the accommodation of the entire party. Swami Brahmananda and Swami Premananda stayed in the same room upstairs. Close to their room there was a spacious decorated parlor. Shortly after his arrival Maharaj was pacing up and down within the parlor. I was standing close to one of the walls. I heard him saying a number of times, "Is it not a shame for a holy man to stay in such a gorgeous place!" After a while I went back where I lived.

Next morning I came again. Swami Premananda and Swami Brahmananda were seated in their room. As I entered the room Swami Premananda introduced me to Maharaj, saying, "This is the boy who has worked hard to secure the permanent site for our Math and Mission Center here."

Maharaj remarked, "Yes, I know him."

Swami Premananda said, "How? You were not at the Math when he was there last summer."

I said, "But I had seen Maharaj at the Math at least twice before."

Maharaj turned to me and said, "Can you find a place for us?" "Yes, Maharaj, it is all for you," I promptly said.

He simply smiled. I did not understand at the time what he meant. Later it occurred to me that he meant whether I could accept him. This is an instance of how even in ordinary conversation his words had much deeper meaning than we realized at the time.

After the arrival of Maharaj and his party at Agnes Villa there was a continuous flow of visitors, including women and students. They wanted to meet one or another of the senior Swamis and talk to them.

One evening a stalwart gentleman of high position came to see the Maharaj who was then seated in his room. The conversation turned to the necessity for the spiritual way of living. The gentleman said that our lives are so full of obstacles that we see no possibility of living a spiritual life. Then Maharaj said, "Pray to the Lord for His grace. Through His grace mountain-high obstacles will disappear like a heap of ash." These encouraging words made the gentleman very happy.

A number of high school and college age students were

drawn to Swami Premananda, who was invited to speak before the students in a college hostel.

Maharaj had a special liking for music, particularly for devotional songs and the chanting of hymns and prayers. In his party there were invariably a few expert musicians, such as Swami Ambikananda, who was a well-trained and talented singer, and Gosai Maharaj (Swami Chidananda), who used to play with his hands on a pair of drums in accompaniment. Within a few days of his coming to Dacca Maharaj exhorted his party and the earnest local devotees to sing Sri Ramnama Sankirtan or Kali Kirtanam in chorus in the evening. Maharaj also told me to join the party. This continued for at least two weeks. There was a special reason why Maharaj wanted the singing of these choral songs (Kirtanam) at the time. He told me about this later in Calcutta.

Knowing his interest in instrumental music we made arrangements for concerts by local expert musicians. An eminent player on the sitar at Dacca, Bhagavan Das, who was a neighbor of mine, gladly came at our request to Agnes Villa and played on the sitar before Maharaj. Another professional musician was asked to play on the usual pair of drums in accompaniment. Maharaj listened to the music with rapt attention.

When the playing was over Maharaj remarked, "As if the divine sage Narada had come down from heaven playing on his harp." Bhagavan Das was of fair complexion with a long beard, and appeared very much like the traditional divine sage Narada, who played on a harp as he travelled from place to place. His younger brother, Shyam Das, was an expert player on another stringed instrument, the esraj. He also came one evening and played before Maharaj. There was music on the drums in accompaniment by the same player as before.

One afternoon Maharaj visited the rented house where the Ramakrishna Math and Mission Center of Dacca was located at the time. A probationer, Satindra Chakravarty (who later became well-known as Swami Gnaneswarananda) was arranging for the evening aratrikam (vesper service). Maharaj expressed a desire to do the vesper. Satindra made the necessary preparations and Maharaj performed the vesper service with the waving of light, etc.

Another day Maharaj and several of his party were invited by Jatin Babu to attend the weekly meeting of the Ramakrishna Association held every Saturday evening at Mohini Babu's house. After the reading of the *Gospel of Sri Ramakrishna* there was a discussion on a relevant topic, followed by a speech by Swami Madhavananda and devotional songs.

Maharaj felt tired. From the assembly hall he came to my room by the adjoining porch. He sat on the bedstead which I used. The bed had been rolled up, and only the underlying mat was on the cot. A close friend of mine, who was very devoted to Maharaj, promptly spread a fresh blanket and Maharaj reclined on it for a little while. Next to the bedroom there was a small shrine-room that I used. Maharaj must have noticed this.

After the meeting of the Association was over, Maharaj and his party were sumptuously fed by the host. Maharaj especially liked two kinds of Hindu sweets (amriti and pantua), for which Dacca had a good reputation and which were supplied by the best caterers of the city.

While at Dacca Maharaj laid the foundation stone of the Ramakrishna Math, and Swami Premananda laid the foundation stone of the Ramakrishna Mission at the permanent site. Appropriate ritualistic worship was performed on the occasion by Swami Ambikananda and others according to Maharaj's instruction.

After the ceremony was over Maharaj and his party, and a considerable number of local devotees, were entertained with a noontime dinner in the house of Thakur Charan Mukherjee, who was then Secretary of the Ramakrishna Math and Mission at Dacca, and who lived in a rented house close by.

One afternoon Maharaj visited Vijay-krishna Goswami's ashrama at Dacca accompanied by Swami Premananda and a few others of his party. I had the privilege of being with them. In a quiet place there stood a small brick-built temple where daily worship was performed by one of the lay devotees who lived in an adjacent home. On the temple grounds there was a hut with a porch where Maharaj and Swami Premananda sat. On receiving the information of their arrival several lay devotees came from the neighborhood to meet them. After a short conversation Maharaj and his party left. Vijay-krishna Goswami's mother-in-law, who saw Sri Ramakrishna, was not there at the time.

It occurred to me later that the purpose of Maharaj's visit was to pay respects to the memory of Vijay-krishna Goswami, who met Sri Ramakrishna a number of times and had great veneration for him. While Maharaj was at Vrindavan during his itinerant days, around 1890, Vijay-krishna Goswami was also living there at the time, and treated Maharaj very affectionately, knowing him to be the beloved spiritual son of Sri Ramakrishna. Noticing that Maharaj had no mosquito curtain, Vijay-krishna Goswami brought one and fixed it over Maharaj's bed to prevent him from being molested at night by the swarms of mosquitos with which Vrindavan was infested.

One day I expressed to Maharaj my earnest desire to enter into monastic life. He told me to take care of my mother as long as she lived because there was no one else to look after her. "Do not be impatient. You have to observe two things — truthfulness and continence," he urged. Other than this he did not impose any disciplinary course on me.

Maharaj was graciously willing to give initiation to a number of earnest local devotees, both men and women.

One day I approached Maharaj for spiritual instruction. He told me to wait and see him at Belur Math. Then he added, "You continue to do what you have been doing. You will have a new life." From my early youth I used to sit regularly twice a day for prayer and meditation and scriptural reading. I was not sure whether I was proceeding rightly and making any progress. I had not told Maharaj anything about it. Therefore, his remark "You will have a new life" made a deep impression on me.

I used to study Sanskrit scriptures and philosophical works from the beginning of my college days (autumn of 1907) with the help of orthodox Sanskrit scholars who did not know English. Since Maharaj said "You will have a new life," I noticed I had greater and greater penetration into the meanings of the scriptures. Some months later one morning as I was meditating, the significance of the following verse of the *Bhagavad Gita* was all of a sudden open unto me.

> Of the unreal there is no being, of the Real there is no non-being. The culmination of both have been found by the seers of Truth.   (II:16)

It was manifest to me that the same truth was declared by Gaudapada (teacher of Shankara's teacher, Govindapada), in his *Mandukya-Karika* (versified exposition of the *Mandukya Upanishad)* in the following verse (II:6):

> That which is non-existent in the beginning and in the end is so in the present (manifest state) also. Such are apparent like the illusions, still they are looked upon as real.

From Dacca, Maharaj, Swami Premananda and several others went for a few days to Kashimpur at the invitation of Sarada Babu, the owner of Agnes Villa, who usually lived in his suburban home. I was not able to join the party.

Before leaving for Calcutta Maharaj and Swami Premananda, along with a party of monks and devotees, paid a day's visit to Deobhog, the birth-place of Sadhu Nag Mahasaya. There both Maharaj and Swami Premananda were in rapturous delight. Unfortunately, I could not accompany them because of my commitments, including attendance on my mother, who was not well.

They went to Deobhog via Narayangunj, the nearest railway station from Dacca, where they were to board the passenger steamer next day on the way to Calcutta. They passed the previous night in a devotee's home at Narayangunj. That same evening, accompanied by a senior devotee, I went there from Dacca to tender our parting salutations at their feet. They reached Belur Math toward the end of February, 1916, before the celebration of Sri Ramakrishna's birth anniversary.

While at Dacca I was told by Maharaj to see him at Belur Math, but I could not make it until June (1916). There I approached Maharaj for initiation at the earliest opportunity. He told me to wait and not to be impatient. Meanwhile my mind wavered; I decided to go to Jayrambati to receive initiation from Holy Mother. I also took leave of Maharaj on the eve of my trip, but my plan did not succeed. I have recorded the whole story of the trip in my reminiscences of Holy Mother, so I shall not repeat the same here.

On my return I saw Maharaj again with trepidation in my heart, but Maharaj, who meanwhile had heard about the failure of my plan, did not take the slightest offense. Rather, he treated me as tenderly as before. As soon as he saw me he said in Sanskrit, "Many are the obstacles on the way to Supreme Good." This and other incidents convinced me that he was the one who could love others, not in spite of, but with their faults.

I ventured to approach Maharaj again for initiation. He said, "Wait, I have to see the almanac to find an auspicious day. It is not an easy thing to give initiation. I have to work hard." The next time I approached Maharaj the result was the same. This happened two or three times.

Once he told me to go and ask for Swami Premananda's permission. As I approached Swami Premananda for permission he said, "It all depends on Maharaj. If he graciously gives you initiation you are fortunate."

Finally Maharaj gave me spiritual instruction and told me to follow the course regularly, and see him again on his return from his trip to Southern India. I lived at Belur Math as long as Maharaj was there. I used to be in close touch with him as far as possible.

One morning after strolling on the lawn for a while Maharaj was seated under the Vilva tree in front of Swamiji's memorial temple. I was standing close by. Maharaj said, "When I am in Benares do not come to me for initiation. I do not give initiation in Benares. There Viswanath, the presiding deity of Benares, is the only guru."

Another day he was standing near the fence of the lawn on which the cows were grazing at some distance. One of the cows called Lakshmi was very fond of him. At the sight of Maharaj, the cow ran to him. He reached over the fence and patted her. I was standing close by. Maharaj told me, "She likes bananas." I asked, "Shall I get some bananas?" "That would be fine," he said.

At once I ran to the market which was nearly three miles away. When I came back with about a dozen bananas Maharaj was still waiting there, and the cow was standing close to him. I handed the bananas to Maharaj. He held out the bananas to the cow. She gulped them.

Late in the afternoon, Maharaj was found seated on the big bench on the ground floor verandah of the original Math building, facing the Ganges. This building provided the only residential quarters of the Belur Monastery at the time. I usually stood at one end of the big bench very close to Maharaj, or sat on the narrow bench opposite to his.

At sunset Maharaj invariably asked the attendant Swami to bring him a little Ganges water and pour it in the palms of his hands. Maharaj rubbed his palms with Ganges water and then sat for a while in deep meditation with folded hands. Like Sri Ramakrishna, Maharaj had deep regard for Ganges water and the Maha Prasad of Jagannath at Puri.

One day as I was standing at one end of the big bench close to Maharaj, a funny incident took place. A young man of Mymensingh, who had come to the monastery to spend his summer vacation in the company of holy men, came to Maharaj to take leave of him. His holiday was over, and he was getting ready to go back home.

During his stay, Maharaj had noticed that the young man had been particularly devoted to Swami Premananda, who was the center of attraction for many ardent visitors in those days.

With his characteristic sense of humour and love of fun, Maharaj took this opportunity to have a little fun at the expense of his brother-disciple, Swami Premananda. After the young man had bowed down at the feet of Maharaj, Maharaj said, "Have you taken leave of Baburam Maharaj [Swami Premananda]?"

"No, Maharaj, not yet," the young man replied. "I am going to take leave of him now."

"Well, when you bow down to him you should say the *pranama-mantra* [salutation formula]. Perhaps you do not know this, but I shall teach you!"

So saying, Maharaj began to recite a Bengali couplet which he quite probably improvised at the time. Freely translated, it ran something like this: "My mind is reluctant to go back home; it is my earnest desire to lie down forever at those holy feet."

Then Maharaj instructed him how to act while saying the mantra. He told him that he should first stand before Swami Premananda with hands folded in great veneration, and then repeat the couplet until he came to the line: "To lie down forever at *those* holy feet." While repeating the line he was to direct his still folded hands toward the Swami's feet, and then bow down.

As the young man left, Maharaj told me to follow him and watch. Swami Premananda was then seated on a bench in the back porch of the building. I saw the young man standing before Swami Premananda with folded hands as Maharaj had instructed him, but he was mute. However, as he bowed down, the Swami noticed that he was mumbling something at his feet, and asked: "What is this? What are you saying? Speak out, my boy!" But the boy remained silent. And then I laughed. Hearing me laugh, Swami Premananda turned to me and said: "Ah! You know what he is saying, surely! Please tell me!" And then I told him the whole story of the *pranama-mantra,* and when I had finished he could not restrain his smile. "Maharaj makes fun like a young boy," he said.

Toward the end of July, Maharaj and his party left for Madras for an extensive tour in southern India.

After my return to Dacca I followed Maharaj's instructions scrupulously.

On his way back from Madras Maharaj stayed in Puri at Balaram Bose's house (Sashi-niketan — close to the ocean beach) with Swami Turiyananda, who was seriously ill and had undergone a major operation on his hand and leg. During his stay in Puri Maharaj visited Bhubaneswar, and secured a large plot of land in order to establish a Math center there. For the facility of Swami Turiyananda's medical treatment it was necessary to bring him to Calcutta while he was bedfast.

Maharaj made all necessary arrangements for his transference and arrived with him in Calcutta in the early part of November, 1917. Both of them were accommodated in the Udbodhan House at Baghbazar where Holy Mother used to live under the care of Swami Saradananda. She was then at Jayrambati, her birth-place. Swami Saradananda's room upstairs was vacated for Swami Turiyananda. Maharaj was accommodated in the office room downstairs. There he used to sleep and meet visitors as well.

On receiving the news that Maharaj had returned to Calcutta I went from Dacca to see him. From the railway station I went direct to Udbodhan House instead of going to Belur Math. As I was going to enter Maharaj's room Swami Dhirananda — a senior monk and disciple of Holy Mother — saw me. Being in charge of the Dacca center he was kindly disposed to me. He thought I was shy and not bold enough to tell Maharaj my difficulties. So of his own accord he came forward and said to Maharaj, pointing to me, "He has some questions."

As I saw Maharaj seated on a chair I bowed down at his feet, touched them and sat down on the floor. Maharaj looked upon me graciously and said, "You have seen a holy man, have bowed down to him and touched his feet, what more questions can there be?" Evidently he meant that this was enough to solve my problems and remove all doubts and difficulties from within. Truly speaking I did not have any question to ask. I only came to see Maharaj.

Like Sri Ramakrishna he had the power to transmit spirituality by a look, by a touch, by a word, by a wish. I knew this from my own experience and from what I had heard from others. I have already mentioned that at Dacca Maharaj once said to me, "You will have a new life." From then on I definitely felt an inner transformation, as I have noted already.

After paying my respects to Maharaj I went upstairs to see Swami Turiyananda, who was bedridden. As far as I can remember I also went to Balaram Bose's house to see Swami Premananda, who was sick in bed. Then I went to Belur Math, my destination.

From there I used to come almost everyday to Calcutta particularly to see Maharaj. I used to sit in Maharaj's presence in his room on the floor. In those days Maharaj very often spoke of Bhubaneswar, where he had secured an extensive lot for establishing a Math. He spoke very highly of the spiritual atmosphere of Bhubaneswar, which besides being conducive to the inner development of monks, would also serve as an adjacent health resort for monastic workers at Belur Math, who often suffered from malaria and had to be sent to far off places for a change.

One morning Swami Saradananda came to Maharaj to report Swami Turiyananda's condition to him. He was carrying a chart regarding his temperature, medication, diet, etc., and was standing beside the cot on which Maharaj was seated. Maharaj said to him, "Sit down Sarat, sit down." When Maharaj repeated this, Swami Saradananda, as if in obedience to his wish, picked up the corner of the mattress and sat on the bare cot. He did not think himself worthy of sitting on the same mattress as Maharaj. This is an instance of the great veneration with which his brother-disciples held him.

One day I had an opportunity to remind Maharaj of my expectation of initiation. He told me to wait.

I had also the blessed privilege of visiting Dakshineswar with Maharaj. It came about this way: one morning at the Udbodhan House as I was seated on the floor before Maharaj in his room, I heard him saying to a devotee, "I want to see the Divine Mother at Dakshineswar today. Please come with your car in the afternoon about 3:00 P.M." After hearing this I took prompt steps to go to Dakshineswar, because it was a unique opportunity to be there with Maharaj. I reached there before 3:00 P.M. and was waiting near the gate for his arrival.

When Maharaj got out of the car he saw me standing by the road inside the temple ground waiting for his arrival, and asked me how I had come. I replied that I had come by ferry boat. He said, "A big steam-launch is bringing the sadhus from Belur Math. It can carry 100 passengers. When you go back be sure to return by the steam-launch." I felt elated.

Then to my surprise, several motor cars came one after another. In one Swami Saradananda came with his devotees. In another Swami Akhandananda came with his devotees. Then several other devotees came in their cars. Very soon the steam-launch arrived with a large number of monastics from Belur Math. About a hundred persons had gathered by this time.

It was beyond my expectation, because I thought that Maharaj had planned the visit only for himself. The devotees brought with them baskets of confections, fruits, and flowers as offerings for the Kali temple and the Vishnu temple. As far as I can remember it was the day of the worship of the Divine Mother Jagaddhatri. Maharaj had brought from Madras a beautiful Madrasi sari for the Divine Mother and had sent it beforehand to Ramlal Dada, the priest. One of the objects of this visit was to see how the Divine Mother appeared decorated with the sari.

As Maharaj and his party stood before the shrine, not only the western door, which was usually kept open for visitors, but the northern door also was opened to permit more daylight into the sanctum sanctorum. So we all had a clear view of the Divine Mother, Bhavatarini, beautifully decorated with a silk sari. Swami Akhandananda sat in front of the temple and chanted hymns, with his face glowing with devotion.

Then the whole party walked behind the Maharaj as he went from the Kali temple to the Vishnu temple, and then to the Shiva temples. Then we followed him to Sri Ramakrishna's room. There Maharaj and his brother-disciples sat for a short time, with as many as could enter the room. Then Maharaj visited the Panchavati and the Bel tree with a paved bottom.

But nowhere did Maharaj speak out a single word.

Swami Saradananda and Swami Akhandananda walked behind him, others followed. No one uttered a single word. The whole party moved like a silent pageant. We expected to hear from Maharaj many incidents regarding his close association with Sri Ramakrishna at Dakshineswar during the most formative period of his life. But it seemed his heart was too full for words.

Meanwhile offered fruits and sweets were distributed to the gathering. It proved to be a great festive occasion. Before evening Maharaj and his brother Swamis went back to Calcutta with the retinue of devotees. I returned to Belur Math in the steam-launch with the sadhus who came from there.

One afternoon I had the privilege of a pleasant trip with Maharaj and his party along the Ganges on the same steam-launch. As far as I remember Maharaj came from the Udbodhan Office at Baghbazar to Belur Math on the steam launch, accompanied by a number of devotees. His purpose was to include some monastics from Belur Math in the party. Fortunately, I was taken on board the steamer along with the monastics.

The steam-launch belonged to the estate of Coochbihar. Sourjyendu Babu, who was very devoted to Maharaj, had a respectable position in the estate. He secured the steam-launch for the use of the Maharaj and the monastics. The steam-launch went down along the river towards Diamond Harbor, the chief port of Calcutta on the Bay of Bengal. We enjoyed the view of Calcutta and the suburbs on both sides of the river. At the same time offered fruits and sweets were distributed among the passengers. We returned before sunset.

As I sat before Maharaj on the floor in his room at the Udbodhan House, I noticed on some days devotees came to him for consultation on different matters. There was one Kshirode-prasad Vidyavinode, Professor of Metropolitan College, who had written a drama on Ramanuja. He used to come with his manuscript and read out to Maharaj for suggestions for improvement. While listening Maharaj suggested alterations here and there. Some came with the blueprints of their building plans to consult Maharaj on some crucial points.

These and similar incidents reminded me of Sri Ramakrishna's remark to Swami Vivekananda, "Rakhal has raja-buddhi [lit. the intelligence of a king]." Truly, he had the administrative capacity of a ruler, and could give practical instruction on a great variety of subjects.

I used to come from Belur Math and see Maharaj and Swami Premananda as often as I could, but I had to lose much time in crossing the river by ferry-boat. It was not very convenient, so I decided to stay in Calcutta with the permission of Swami Shivananda, who was then in charge of the Belur Monastery. I went to the Vivekananda Society located in a rented apartment on the second floor of a building on a crowded street. Swami Shuddhananda,* one of the earliest and most erudite of the disciples of Swami Vivekananda, was in charge, and lived there. I was well

*Swamiji set him to the task of translating *Raja-Yoga* into Bengali. This was the first of Swami Vivekananda's works to appear in Bengali. Swami Shuddhananda also translated into Bengali most of Swamiji's lectures delivered in India. The volume appeared under the title *Bharate Vivekananda* (Vivekananda in India).

acquainted with him at Dacca.

As I came to him and told him my difficulty, he was willing to make arrangements for my meals there. But I was to sleep at night on the high reading room table. As customary in India I had taken my bedding with me, and I gladly agreed to this arrangement. There were only two small bedrooms, one of which was used by Swami Shuddhananda, and the other by the attendant Brahmachari (Taranath). So I left my bedding there and came to Balaram Bose's house, which was not far.

This was an extensive two-storied building constructed on four sides of a rectangular open court. The main residential section (including guest bedrooms, a large drawing room, officers' kitchen block, Ramakrishna Bose's office room and ladies quarters) was on the second floor. Attached to the second floor there were covered porches in front of the building, and also inside the building on the four sides of the inner court. On the first floor there were a number of guest bedrooms.

Shortly after my arrival there Swami Shuddhananda came and went to the office-room of Ramakrishna Bose, the worthy son of Balaram Bose. He spoke to him about me by way of introduction, and said that I had come from Dacca with the main object of seeing Maharaj and receiving initiation from him, and that I had been to the Vivekananda Society for accommodation. On hearing him, Ramakrishna Bose (who was a disciple of Maharaj as far as I know) promptly came forward to me in the drawing room and said, "How can you live away from the company? Please bring your bedding and live here." Needless to say, I was exceedingly happy and at once followed what he said.

Most of the monastic workers who attended on the venerable Swamis — Brahmananda, Premananda, Turiyananda, and Akhandananda — used to have their meals at Balaram Bose's house and also slept there at night. Swami Akhandananda lived there at the time. About eight of us, including Swami Akhandananda, used to sleep in the same long drawing room, each on a separate narrow bed with individual mosquito curtains. Some nights at bedtime I joined with the personal attendant of Swami Akhandananda to massage his legs and feet. The Swami had a stout body.

Swami Premananda was lying on a sick bed in the bedroom to the west of the long drawing room. It was the same bedroom in which Sri Ramakrishna used to sleep whenever he spent the night in Calcutta. At other times the same bedroom was used by Maharaj, who frequently lived at Balaram Bose's house. The bedroom and the extensive drawing room occupied the entire front wing of the second floor. The ladies' section was in the back wing of the house opposite to the front wing. The officers' kitchen block was on the side wing between the front and the back wings.

Excepting Swami Akhandananda, all other guests used to have their meals with the officers of the Balaram Bose estate in the kitchen block managed by a paid cook and servant. Occasionally homemade desserts prepared by the ladies in the inner section of the house were sent for us all. Sometimes Ramakrishna Bose would come forward and announce ahead of time the coming of a special dessert.

Balaram Bose's house was only a few blocks away from Udbodhan House. Both were located in the same neighborhood called Baghbazar. Almost every morning Maharaj used to walk up to Balaram Bose's house from Udbodhan House and spend about three or four hours there. His main purpose was to see Swami Premananda and to meet the devotees in the drawing room. Very often he had an invitation to dinner in the ladies' quarters.

One day as I was seated close to Maharaj in the drawing room Lalit Babu came, whom Maharaj called "Kaiser" (because of his beard shaven like that of the Kaiser of the first World War). He had undertaken the collection of funds for the building of Holy Mother's memorial temple on her birthplace at Jayrambati. On seeing me he said, "You devotees of Dacca, why do you not collect funds for building the temple on the Holy Mother's birthplace at Jayrambati?" I felt shy, because I did not have the knack to do this kind of work. Maharaj looked at me and said, "No, no, he cannot do this." I felt relieved.

Then Lalit Babu, in order to turn away Maharaj's attention, pointed to the oil painting of Sri Ramakrishna hanging on the wall behind Maharaj, and said, "Maharaj, was Thakur like this?" Maharaj looked back at the picture and kept silent and became very grave as if he was too full to say anything about Sri Ramakrishna. We observed the same intense feeling when we visited Dakshineswar with him.

Maharaj was fond of children. Two young daughters of Ramakrishna Bose, about ten and eight years old, Mahamaya and Yogamaya, would invariably come out to the front wing to see Maharaj. He used to have fun with them and often gave them tidbits. One day as the girls were approaching, Maharaj appeared to them with the mask of a tiger on his face. The girls fled and looked back from a distance. Maharaj took off the mask. The girls laughed and said, "You are very naughty, Maharaj."

One morning as Maharaj came to Balaram Bose's house, walking from Udbodhan House, his legs felt tired. He sat down on the floor of the drawing room and extended his legs. With his permission, I had the opportunity to massage his legs and feet for a few minutes. Maharaj encouraged me to take daily physical exercise. He even approved of my going to the native gymnasium.

Then Lalit Babu came and found me seated close to Maharaj. He scolded me saying, "What kind of devotees are you at Dacca? You kept Maharaj and his party in a haunted house." Then he asked Maharaj to tell me the story of the haunted house. Maharaj related the following incident.

While he stayed at Agnes Villa at Dacca it so happened that on the second day of his being there, as he was seated on his bed at early dawn, he noticed in a corner of his room a very wretched looking, half-naked Mohammedan ghost. A day or two later he had come to know that the young son of Sarada Babu, the owner of Agnes Villa, had committed suicide in that very house a few months before by drinking opium, on being severely scolded by his father for failing in his High School final examination. Close to Agnes Villa there was a mosque. Maharaj had surmised that this ghost had come from its cemetery and persuaded the young boy to commit suicide. Swami Premananda also used to sleep in the same bedroom but he did not see the ghost.

At Dacca, Maharaj did not tell others anything about the ghost, but he asked his party and other devotees to organize Sri Ramnama Kirtanam and Sri Kali-Kirtanam alternately in the evening. One afternoon I came to see Maharaj. He told me to come back in the evening and participate in the Kirtanam. Several days after this the ghost disappeared. Those who participated in the Kirtanam knew nothing about Maharaj's ulterior object in having the choral songs.

One day in the drawing room at Balaram Bose's house, Maharaj told me to bring letter-paper, pen and inkwell from Ramakrishna Bose's office. It is to be noted that in those days a fountain pen was not so common. Then Maharaj wanted me to write a letter in English. "You write as I dictate and wherever possible improve the language," he said. I wrote as he dictated. The letter was addressed — "To the Abbot of Belur Monastery." It can be summarized as follows:

"As customary in your monastery you will no doubt celebrate the annual Christmas Eve festival. We, a party of monks, have been eagerly awaiting your festival. Your hospitality is well-known. After the festival you will no doubt serve palatable food and drink. We are not vegetarians. We eat chops, cutlets and so forth. We offer you hearty thanks in anticipation of a sumptuous dinner. No doubt your festival will be quite successful." Here, with Maharaj's permission, I made a slight change — "No doubt your festival will be crowned with success."

When I had finished writing the letter he signed the name of Swami Premananda instead of his own name. Then he told me to go to Swami Premananda's room and let him read the letter. I did as he said. After reading the letter and

seeing that Maharaj had forged his name, Swami
Premananda smiled and said, "Maharaj has a child-like
nature." I came back to Maharaj and reported to him what
Swami Premananda had said. Then the Maharaj told me to
take the letter to Swami Shivananda at Belur Math. The
letter was addressed "To the Abbot of Belur Monastery." He
told me not to say who had written the letter.

I went to Belur Math and handed it to Swami
Shivananda. After reading the letter, Swami Shivananda
looked at me and said, "Maharaj has sent it, is it not?" I did
not say "yes" or "no" but kept silent and simply nodded my
head a little. Swami Shivananda guessed the truth. It is to be
noted that both Swami Premananda and Swami Shivananda were strict vegetarians.

In the same drawing room Maharaj used to tease his
brother-disciple, Swami Akhandananda, who was younger.
He was a stout person and of simple nature. After the
passing of Sri Ramakrishna he went out as an itinerant
monk to many places of pilgrimage in Northern India and in
the Himalayas. He also crossed the Himalayas and went to
Tibet and stayed there with the Lamas about three years.
Inspired by Swamiji's ideal of serving God in man he had
started an orphanage at Sargachi near Murshidabad, West
Bengal. From Sargachi he had come to Calcutta this time
especially in order to see Swami Premananda during his
illness. While in Calcutta he used to go out just like an
itinerant monk with an ochre turban and a long ochre robe.
This dress was a gift of Maharaj as far as I know.

In order to purchase slippers and other petty things for
the small orphan boys he himself would go out dressed in his

monastic garb. Maharaj always discouraged him saying,
"Brother, let one of the Brahmacharis here go out and buy
these things for the boys. Why do you go yourself?" Yet he
insisted that he should go himself and choose the right
things.

While Swami Akhandananda would get ready to go out
Maharaj would sometimes call one of the Brahmacharis
present and tell him to hide the Swami's turban. After
searching for the turban and not finding it, Swami
Akhandananda would guess that Maharaj had played a
trick on him. Then he would come to Maharaj with tears in
his eyes and say, "Maharaj, you know where my turban is.
Kindly let me have the turban, let me have the turban."
Maharaj would tell him to look for the turban where he had
kept it.

In this way four weeks passed. One morning as I was
seated beside Swami Premananda's sick bed, which was
placed on the floor carpet, he said that it would be proper for
me to go back to Belur Math and stay there, because it was
an imposition on Balaram Bose's estate to live there
continuously. With Maharaj's permission I decided to go
back to Belur Math and stay there. When I begged for
initiation he told me that he would inform me of the day on
which initiation would be given. I went back to Belur Math
and stayed there.

Some days later Swami Shivananda came to Calcutta
to meet his brother Swamis. On his return to Belur Math he
told me, "Maharaj wants you to see him at Balaram Bose's
house on such and such day." He also indicated that it was
for initiation. I came to Maharaj at Balaram Bose's house in

the early morning on the appointed day. It was the auspicious day of Makara Samkranti (the turning up of the sun from the Tropic of Capricorn).*

Maharaj was walking up and down in the drawing room. As indicated by him I sat on the floor. After some time he came to me and sat down on the floor before me. Then he gave me initiation. He gave me the mantra and told me how I should visualize the Chosen Ideal (Ishta) and practice meditation. Then I asked what relationship I should maintain with the Chosen Ideal. He said, "This will develop within you as you follow the spiritual course. He is your all in all." Then I asked him the meaning of the mantra. He said, "There is no difference in the meaning between the mantra and the Chosen Ideal. They mean the same thing. He is your all in all." The one thing that Maharaj urged was the steady and regular practice of the course from day to day.

That day Maharaj had been invited to dine in the women's section. I also went there and was given some prasad. It was after the initiation that I brought him some offerings. Maharaj told me that I should have a rosary. After the dinner I went to Udbodhan House. Maharaj had told Brahmachari Kshudiram (later Swami Shymananda) to buy a rudraksha rosary for me. Maharaj preferred a half rosary of fifty-four beads. After Kshudiram had brought the beads, one of the Swamis who attended on Swami Premananda properly strung the beads. Maharaj took the rosary in his hands, counted the beads and gave it to me with the necessary instruction. Needless to say I have preserved the

*Winter solstice, about December 22, the shortest day of the year.

rosary carefully all along. Then I went to see Swami Premananda lying on his sick bed. He congratulated me and blessed me.

About the middle of January, 1918, I returned to Dacca with the blessings of Maharaj and his brother-disciples. There I participated in Swamiji's birth anniversary at the Ashrama.

While at Dacca I tried to follow the Maharaj's instruction for spiritual practice as far as my capacity and situation in life permitted. The permanent center of the Ramakrishna Math and Mission at Dacca was founded in 1916-17 on the outskirts of the city.

The original Ramakrishna Association, which used to hold its meetings regularly every Saturday evening at the old Mohini Babu's house where Swami Vivekananda stayed, was transferred to a spacious living room on the second floor of an attractive building in the same locality. Being situated in the front section of the building, the living room had free access by a stairway close to the main gate of the house. The owner, a generous friend of mine, offered the use of the room. Further, he built for me a tiny cottage on the third floor which served as my shrine. Previously I lived in a rented house with my mother.

About the middle of June, 1918, I left Dacca accompanied by a friend of mine for a pilgrimage to Puri on the Bay of Bengal, in order to attend a festival there. On my way to Puri I stopped in Calcutta and saw Maharaj at Balaram Bose's house in the same drawing room. He was very happy to know that I was going on a pilgrimage to Puri. He urged me to visit Bhubaneswar temple, which was then under construction.

Swami Shankarananda with four monastic assistants was supervising the work. I had carried with me a basket of a special type of imported mangoes as an offering which he appreciated very much. He told the Swami who used to attend on him to soak the mangoes in cold water. In a short while Chuni Babu, who had seen Sri Ramakrishna, and whom Sri Ramakrishna called "Narayan," came to see Maharaj. Then I left.

I lived in Puri about two weeks. I fully utilized my stay there. I visited the temple of Jagannath according to the orthodox Hindu custom. I had the privilege of seeing "Gambhira," a tiny room where Sri Chaitanya lived with his two attending disciples, mostly in a state of ecstacy during the last eighteen years of his life. I also paid my respects to the various other temples of the Hindu community including the Govardhan Math founded by Padmapada, one of the four main disciples of Sri Shankaracharya. I saw "Sashi-niketan" of Balaram Bose, which was the favorite abode of Maharaj and other disciples of Sri Ramakrishna in Puri. I also enjoyed my daily swim in the ocean.

At the time of this festival I met Swami Shankarananda, who came to Puri with his assistant Swamis to attend the festival. A close friend of mine, Prafulla Banerjee of Dacca also came. Accompanied by him I stopped in Bhubaneswar on my way back to Calcutta, and stayed at the Ashrama four days with the permission of Swami Shankarananda. At that time the main building had been constructed up to the top of the front columns intended to support the arches. Swami Shankarananda and his assistants lived in the kitchen and dining quarters over which a thatched roof was built temporarily. They had their bedrooms there. My friend and I were accommodated in one of the rooms.

At first I went to the main Bhubaneswar temple dedicated to Shiva. It was very lofty and of special architectural design. All over Bhubaneswar there were numerous deserted Shiva temples. Though small, they were of the same architectural design carved in red stone. One of the assistants of Swami Shankarananda took great interest in showing me the various places. We also went to the top of the hills Khandagiri and Udayagiri.

After staying at Bhubaneswar about four days I came back to Calcutta, and saw Maharaj at Balaram Bose's house and reported my visit to Puri and Bhubaneswar to him. He was very happy to hear about it. At that time Swami Premananda was at Deoghar for a change. During my stay in Calcutta I came to see Maharaj every day. One day Maharaj gave me further instruction for spiritual practice. He told me to practice "purascharana" (the regular measure of japa and meditation at one sitting). For one year I was to practice short puruscharana and the next year the long purascharana. I was also told to eat strictly vegetarian food, one meal a day, preferably cooked by myself. In the evening I was to eat a light supper consisting of fruits and one or two sweets.

I stayed in Calcutta about a week on my way back to Dacca and visited Maharaj daily at Balaram Bose's house. One day after his noonday meal at Balaram Bose's house he had a siesta in the drawing room. Shortly after that I came and was seated near the Maharaj's bed. About the same time

Golap Ma, a constant companion of the Holy Mother, who attended on her most devotedly, entered the room.

She related to Maharaj an account of the festival that was held in the house of Dr. Kanjilal, who had invited a number of sadhus from Belur Math on the occasion. Golap Ma told Maharaj that he had given personal gifts to the sadhus and had sent a number of metal vessels of different sizes to Belur Math. As she was describing the vessels with her hands she remarked, "He [Dr. Kanjilal] is doing all these things, but his nature is not changing." She referred to Dr. Kanjilal's habit of tyrannizing his wife. Maharaj at once became very grave and said, "Golap Ma, you will not understand this."

Dr. Kanjilal was one of the few devotees who used to come to Maharaj very often. They were all men of good position and were very devoted to Maharaj. In spite of their wrong habits Maharaj harbored them because of their sincerity. Maharaj did not always instruct them on spiritual truths. He often cut jokes with them. Even through these he used to impart spiritual and moral lessons.

I do not recall the stories I heard. Only one story which was reported to me comes to my mind, about how a clever person can vitiate moral and spiritual lessons. Once a man came to the law court. The prosecutor asked him his age. "My age is 43," he said. Then the prosecutor said, "Five years ago you came to this court. Then also you said that you were 43 years old. How can that be?" He answered, "A gentleman must keep his word."

From Calcutta I returned to Dacca around the middle of July, 1918. Swami Premananda passed away on July 30, a few days after his return from Deoghar. The sad news reached me duly.

I practiced the light purascharana methodically week after week for one full year, strictly according to Maharaj's instruction. I also used to cook my mid-day meal. My mother partook of the same food. In the evening I used to take only fruits and one or two sweets.

The following year I practiced long purascharana week after week methodically. Most probably I was occupied with the practice of the two courses of purascharana from the autumn of 1918 to the autumn of 1920. Early in the winter of 1920 I went on a pilgrimage with a friend of mine to the Northwestern Province of India and the Himalayas.

Maharaj was then staying at the Bhubaneswar temple, which was dedicated by him in 1919 at the time of the Durga Puja festival. Before going out on the pilgrimage I wrote to Maharaj for his permission and blessings. For visiting holy places permission is not necessary he indicated in his reply.

With my friend's party I went directly to Hardwar. From there I, by myself, walked to Kankhal Sevashrama and met Swami Kalyanananda, the founder-head of the ashrama. He received me very cordially as an old acquaintance. I felt at home. From Kankhal I went to Hrisikesh. From there I walked as far as Lachhmanjhola, the suspension bridge, on the Ganges on the way to the Badarika Ashrama. On my way back from Hardwar I visited Vrindavan, Ajodhya, and Benares with my friend's party. I also made a trip to Allahabad with the main object of diving into the confluence of the Ganges and the Jamuna.

We arrived in Benares in December, 1920. After a short

stay there my friend and his party went back to Calcutta on the way to Dacca. I stayed in Benares and attended the Christmas Eve celebration at Benares Sevashrama (Home of Service) held in the spacious office room. Swami Shuddhananda spoke on the occasion. We were told that Maharaj would come to Benares in January, 1921. We were awaiting his arrival. I considered it a rare blessing to be in Benares with Maharaj.

I met Chandra Baba, who was the head of the Ramakrishna Advaita Ashrama in Benares.. Swami Gnaneswarananda, a friend from my youth who was living there, introduced me to Chandra Baba and then to Swami Shantananda, one of the senior resident Swamis there. Chandra Baba permitted me to stay in the Advaita Ashrama. I was accommodated in a single room. I was happy to meet Prabhu Maharaj (later Swami Vireswarananda) at the Advaita Ashrama. He, too, was awaiting Maharaj's arrival.

Shortly after my arrival in Benares I went to see Swami Turiyananda, who was living in the Sevashrama special quarters reserved for the senior guest Swamis. As in Calcutta, so in Benares, Sanat Maharaj (Swami Prabodhananda) was his personal attendant. Swami Yatiswarananda served as his personal secretary. During my stay in Benares I, along with several Swamis and Brahmacharis, used to go every morning and sit at the feet of Swami Turiyananda and listen to his words of wisdom. One morning we heard the following incident concerning his early days, which distinguishes the apostles of Sri Ramakrishna, the living free souls, from the seekers of liberation in general.

In the words of Swami Turiyananda, "One day as I visited Thakur [the Divine Master — Sri Ramakrishna] he asked me, 'Well, Hari [his family name was Harinath Chattopadhyaya], what do you want?' 'Moksha,' I forthwith replied. 'You are small-minded,' he rejoined. I looked at him in wonderment; I thought within myself, do not all Vedanta books proclaim moksha to be the highest goal of life? 'You see,' continued the Master, 'the expert chess players are so sure of winning the game that they deliberately turn down the pieces before reaching the goal in order to continue the play.' The illumined souls know that they are ever free whether they dwell in the body or not, it makes no difference to them. So they are not afraid of being reborn time and again for helping bound souls to attain liberation, but the unillumined seekers are too eager to get free from the round of birth and rebirth."

Swami Turiyananda at the same time pointed out that only a select few among the liberated-in-life, jivanmukta, are capable of dedicating themselves to the Supreme Ideal of helping all living creatures to attain liberation, without seeking final emancipation by merging into the infinite bliss of Brahman. Sri Ramakrishna called these blessed ones "ever free" (nitya-mukti). He included some of his disciples, especially Swami Vivekananda and Swami Brahmananda, in this rank.

Late in the afternoon one of the Swamis (Kamaleswarananda) would read the Bengali translation of the *Srimad Bhagavatam* to Swami Turiyananda. I attended the reading along with other sadhus and devotees. In spite of his ill health Swami Turiyananda would take a walk in the Sevashrama grounds for a while almost every day.

Every morning I went to the Ganges for bathing accompanied by Swami Gnaneswarananda. On the way back I visited the temples of Viswanath (Shiva) and Annapurna. In the afternoon Swami Gnaneswarananda or Swami Shantananda, or both, used to escort me to various notable temples and other holy places in Benares.

As the joyous news of Maharaj's coming to Varanasi, the abode of Shiva, circulated, there was quite an influx of sadhus to this sacred place from various centers of the Ramakrishna Order. Most of them, including the elderly, had not received formal initiation into Sannyas or Brahmacharya. At the same time the message was spread that here in Varanasi Maharaj would admit into formal Sannyas and Brahmacharya Orders deserving candidates on such festive occasions as the birth anniversary of Swami Vivekananda. Many probationer monastics had been staying here from before Maharaj's arrival in expectation of receiving the vows of Sannyas and Brahmacharya. Not a few lay devotees of the Ramakrishna Order also came for the blessed privilege of living here in Maharaj's presence.

Finally the definite information reached us that Maharaj would arrive by railway train from Calcutta in the early morning on the 20th of January, accompanied by Swami Saradananda and his personal attendants. The train would reach Mogul Sari Junction at about 3:00 A.M. The direct local train from Mogul Sari to Varanasi would not be available before morning. Nobody liked the idea of the Maharaj's waiting in an adjacent railway station for about three hours in the morning.

The authorities of the Benares Sevashrama decided to go to Mogul Sari about 3:00 A.M. with motor cars and escort Maharaj and his party to Benares before dawn. Swami Turiyananda, despite his ill-health, left his bed before 3:00 A.M. and got ready to start for Mogul Sari in the car in order to receive Maharaj and his party. Some of us at the Ramakrishna Advaita Ashrama got up very early and were watching from upstairs the starting of the car with Swami Turiyananda and others.

In the early morning Maharaj and his party, including Swami Saradananda, Swami Turiyananda, and the personal attendants, arrived at the gate of Advaita Ashrama in the car. Maharaj and his personal attendants stayed at Advaita Ashrama. Swami Turiyananda and Swami Saradananda were taken to their respective places. We had all eagerly awaited Maharaj's arrival.

For the residence of Maharaj, Chandra Baba had separate living quarters constructed over the kitchen block. There were two spacious rooms, one was meant for Maharaj's bedroom and sitting room, and the other for his attendants and storage. Swami Vishuddhananda, Swami Yatiswarananda, Swami Nirvanananda and also Maharaj's personal attendant, Iswara, made necessary arrangements for his stay.

In the early morning shortly after his arrival, Maharaj was standing on the open porch downstairs of the original building of the Advaita Ashrama near the corner of the kitchen block. We all gathered around him. Some Sevashrama workers came in by the intervening door and were watching the Maharaj from there. Maharaj spoke enthusiastically, "Varanasi is really the abode of Shiva. As soon as our car crossed the bridge over the River Asi and came to the Varanasi side, I felt a complete change of atmosphere in this chosen site of Shiva." (Varanasi is so called being situated at the junction of the two branches of the Ganges, Varuna and Asi.)

We were all watching Maharaj and listening to his words. With the Maharaj's arrival the minds of all were elated with joy. I felt a change in the surrounding atmosphere. From then on continuous festivity went on in Advaita Ashrama from day to day.

During his stay in Varanasi, Maharaj sent money most days to one or another of the major temples such as the Temple of Shiva, Temple of Annapurna, Temple of Durga for the offering of food to the presiding deity. As a matter of course enough prasad (offered food) would be sent from one temple or another at lunch time to the Advaita Ashrama. On account of his physical condition Maharaj had to take a light meal before noontime. When the sadhus of Advaita Ashrama sat in the dining hall for their main meals about noontime, Maharaj would invariably come down and see that each sadhu had been served temple prasad to his satisfaction.

In the early morning we were all permitted to sit for meditation in Maharaj's presence in his room upstairs. Maharaj would be seated on his cot. The sadhus and devotees would sit on the carpeted floor. Those who had special duties in the early morning were not able to come or could not sit long. In the evening the sadhus and devotees were allowed to gather in Maharaj's room and ask questions. Maharaj answered them at length. Three of the Swamis were usually forward in asking questions.

One evening I was late in entering the room. I tried to secure a seat among the monastics who had already filled the room. As I turned from one of the sadhus to another, Maharaj jokingly remarked, "First trace, then you can write. You have to go through preliminary exercises in order to enter the fold."

After Maharaj's arrival the birth anniversary of Swami Vivekananda was held. At dawn Maharaj admitted after due ceremonies about forty probationers into Sannyas and Brahmacharya Orders according to their seniority. A public meeting was held in the afternoon under a canopy fixed in the back yard of the Advaita Ashrama. Swami Saradananda gave an eloquent speech on Sri Ramakrishna and Swamiji in English. A number of professors and students from Benares Hindu University attended the meeting.

As far as I can remember, on the birth anniversary of Maharaj a considerable number of probationers were similarly admitted into Sannyas and Brahmacharya Orders. Before noontime Maharaj was served a sumptuous dinner. He was seated on a decorative mat at one end of the second room in his quarters. Many monastics of Advaita Ashrama and Sevashrama had prepared delicious dishes, and a number of householders brought varieties of food from their homes.

Maharaj put on special dress and was heavily garlanded. Around his plate different kinds of food were arranged on small plates, cups and dishes. Three of the

Swamis sat near the extreme corners of the room. As Maharaj tasted each dish, one of the Swamis removed the dish and another pushed a new plate closer to him.

After Maharaj's meal was over, all the dishes with the remaining food were taken downstairs. Maharaj told the attendants to mix all the food together in a large bowl — curried dishes, dal, curd, sweets, etc. Big balls were made and served to all the sadhus of Advaita Ashrama and Sevashrama, and the devotees who assembled there. They took the lump of food in their joined palms and ate while standing.

Maharaj also arranged Kali Kirtanam at the Temple of Annapurna. Most of the sadhus went in a party and sang in chorus. Sri Ramnama Kirtanam was similarly arranged in the main office room of the Sevashrama, in the Temple of Hanuman, and in the Hermitage of Tulsidas across the River Asi. (The great Saint Tulsidas had his cottage on the other side of Varanasi across the River Asi; because of his humility he did not consider himself worthy of being in the abode of Shiva.) As far as I remember Maharaj and his personal attendants went with the party of singers in the afternoon. I had the blessed privilege of accompanying them one afternoon.

Meanwhile Swami Saradananda was planning to hold a business meeting in the Sevashrama to settle a dispute among the workers and the authorities of the Sevashrama. The dissension had continued for some time past. Swami Saradananda requested Maharaj to attend the meeting at the Sevashrama and settle the differences among the workers and the authorities. He had also framed some rules and regulations with that object in view. But Maharaj delayed. He wanted Swami Saradananda and the others to wait.

Maharaj never did hold the meeting, but his presence and spiritual methods created such an atmosphere that the minds of the dissenters at the Sevashrama were raised to such a high pitch, that they could not think of their quarrel anymore. When the Maharaj left Benares he transferred some of those involved, and some he included in his travelling party, so this was the end of the dissension. Maharaj once remarked, "We usually quarrel on insignificant matters because our minds go down to the lower level."

Meanwhile I had received a letter from my uncle that my mother was very seriously ill, and that I should return home immediately and take care of her. As I have noted already Maharaj told me to take care of my mother as long as she lived. I went to Swami Saradananda to take leave of him. He was living in Kiran Datta's house, which was at the Swami's disposal for the time being.

I expressed my regret to Swami Saradananda that I would have to leave Benares even when Maharaj was there, because Maharaj had told me to look after my mother during her lifetime. I also regretted that my desire to enter into monastic life could not be fulfilled as long as my mother was alive. Swami Saradananda told me that I should do as Maharaj said. Yogin Ma, who occupied the adjoining room, overheard what I had said to Swami Saradananda. She rebuked me severely for looking upon my mother as an obstacle to my being a sadhu.

Finally I went to Maharaj and related to him the letter I

had received from my uncle regarding my mother's serious illness. Maharaj said, "What else can you do. You have to go." Then I told Maharaj, "I do not feel an urge for God, nor do I feel any attachment to the world. Does this mean that I have had wrong tendencies within me?" Maharaj said, "You don't have to worry about that." After this I made arrangements for leaving Benares as soon as possible. I was extremely sad I could not stay in Benares with Maharaj as long as he was there.

In the last week of March, 1922, while staying at Balaram Bose's house, Maharaj became seriously ill. In spite of the best medical care and devoted service of the monastics and devotees, his life could not be spared. It was on the evening of April 10 that Maharaj entered into Mahasamadhi. I had received the news of Maharaj's illness and his fluctuating condition. But my mother was also in a serious condition, and it was not possible for me to leave her.

CHAPTER XI

REMINISCENCES OF SWAMI PREMANANDA

Few great men were as freely accessible as Swami Premananda. I saw him for the first time on Thursday, February 6, 1908, at the headquarters of the Ramakrishna Order at Belur Math, five miles to the northwest of Calcutta, India. I was walking up the steps from the Ganges toward the original monastery building, when I met a venerable Swami coming down the steps. I touched his feet as I bowed down. Then I inquired, "Where is Baburam Maharaj [the popular name of Swami Premananda]?" "Here," he said, pointing to himself, and asked me, "Why?" "The Maharaj [Swami Brahmananda] has told me to see you," I answered. Then Swami Premananda inquired where I had come from and what I had been doing.

From this first meeting until his Mahasamadhi on the 30th July, 1918, I had the privilege of seeing him and being with him in many different places at different times. I cannot recall any extraordinary incident while I was with him, but I cherish the memories of his unique personality as a source of great joy and inspiration.

Although I had visited Belur Monastery a number of times since 1908, I did not spend the night there. It was during the summer vacation in the year 1915 that I had the privilege of living there for the first time. I came with a letter of introduction from the Swami who was in charge of the Ramakrishna Ashrama at Dacca, which was then located in a rented house. As I appeared before Swami Premananda and handed him the letter, he graciously welcomed me and held me in his arms.

What impressed me most during my first stay at Belur Monastery was the great esteem and veneration with which everyone, senior and junior, regarded Swami Premananda. He was looked upon as the very embodiment of divine love and purity. "He is pure to the backbone," said Sri Ramakrishna. His very touch was considered sanctifying. I had no idea before that man could revere man so highly, even though I was born in a family where the elder brother was respected as the father.

As the abbot of the Belur Monastery he did not stay long within his room. He went about the premises several times during the day. It was his practice to observe young monks at work in the kitchen block, storerooms, and shrine, and give them directions. He also used to supervise the yards, the garden, the orchards and the cow sheds.

Besides, he met informally with visitors, who' were mostly strangers and came usually by boat without previous intimation at any time during the day. He received the newcomers as cordially as the old friends. He sat with them very informally on the floor carpet in the visitors' room, or on the benches in the front or the back porch of the original building.

Instead of losing time in formal conversation he spoke to them with great fervor on spiritual ideals and practices, as exemplified in the lives of Sri Ramakrishna, Swami Vivekananda and other illustrious personages. All listened to him with rapt attention. He would hardly talk about anything except God and religion. As pointed out by Sri

Ramakrishna, a distinctive mark of a saint is that he shuns all vain talk and talks only about God. This was quite evident in Swami Premananda.

His mode of living was exceptionally plain and simple. A dhoti, a wrapper, and a pair of brown slippers formed his complete dress. He seldom wore any seamed garment. In deep winter he occasionally used a woolen sweater. He had only a few belongings, and during his trips his attendant carried no suitcase for him, only a canvas bag. The spirit of renunciation was manifest in all his ways. He would hardly allow himself any luxury whatsoever. He was a strict vegetarian, and did not drink tea or coffee, nor did he smoke.

He was of fair complexion with handsome and attractive features. Over and above, he was very affectionate by nature. With motherly feeling he instructed and guided the young monks and novices and was ever-attentive to their needs. Not only did he urge them to practice meditation at regular hours, but also insisted on the right performance of their respective duties, be it worshipping the deity or the paring of vegetables. Even such minor deeds as sweeping the floor or the removal of weeds from the yard was to be done with due attention and accuracy, as an act of worshipping the Lord in taking care of the temple.

In pouring ink from the bottle into the inkwell, not a drop was to be spilled. (It may be noted that in those days pens and inkwells were commonly used instead of fountain pens.) Once I was peeling a special kind of vegetable. Swami Premananda watched and sounded the note of warning, "Much substance is going with the skin." I became alert. He was opposed to waste, no doubt, but he disliked the wrong or the negligent way of doing things even more. He tried to impress on our minds that the test of character was not in glaring performances under the public gaze, but in the quiet and faithful discharge of common duties, unnoticed by others.

Swami Premananda told us that contributions received for charitable and religious purposes ought to be treated as a sacred trust, that it was a great sacrifice on the part of householders to donate what they earned by the sweat of their brow. On no account should their gifts be misused or wasted. Sri Ramakrishna himself considered it a moral crime to waste anything contributed by the devotees for the maintenance of holy men, or for worship or for charitable purposes, insignificant though it might be.

Swami Premananda was equally affectionate toward the lay devotees. Not only did he care for their spiritual enlightenment, but for their material well-being as well. When any of them became sick he would often inquire about their health. Occasionally he sent fruits, vegetables and other produce of the monastery grounds. He found great pleasure in feeding the devotees. Whoever visited the shrine was given offered fruits and sweets.

All those who came to Belur Monastery around noontime were served a mid-day meal along with the monks in the dining hall or the adjoining porch. Swami Premananda often shared with them offered fruits and sweets that were reserved for him beside his plate. In order to feed the latecomers, mostly strangers, sometimes fresh meals had to be cooked even after the kitchen had been cleaned and washed, and the cook and servants had gone for rest. On such occasions Swami Premananda would often go to the kitchen and offer his services to the monastics who took upon themselves the task of cooking fresh meals.

Not only did Swami Premananda urge the monastics to be expert in the normal duties assigned to them, but also encouraged them to be well-equipped with spiritual knowledge. He often mentioned that Swami Vivekananda wanted the monastics to be adept in all types of work, from the mending of shoes to the study of the Vedas.

Every afternoon about 3:00 p.m. most of the young monastics would get together in the visitors' room in the original Math building for the study of the ancient scriptures, and also the teachings of Sri Ramakrishna and Swami Vivekananda. One of the monks used to read the Bengali translation of Sanskrit texts and then a discussion would follow. Swami Premananda would be present at the meeting whenever possible. As far as I can remember Swami Vasudevananda (who later became the editor of the Bengali monthly magazine *Udbodhan*) was very enthusiastic in this respect.

One afternoon an elderly visitor came. He was Pandit Matilal Chakravarty, senior teacher of a well-known vernacular school at Dacca, who knew me. A great admirer of Keshab Chandra Sen, the founder of the Navabidhan Brahmo Samaj, he was fond of making speeches. He was happy to find me at the Math and wanted me to introduce him to Swami Premananda. I took him to Swami Premananda, who was then at the class.

Swami Premananda received the Pandit cordially and

asked him to give some instruction to the monastic students, but the Pandit hesitated to open his mouth before Swami Premananda and requested him, on the contrary, to talk to the monastic group. He was well impressed with Swami Premananda's cordial reception and enthusiastically spoke to me about the Swami's blessings when he met me long after his return to Dacca.

One day Swami Premananda was seated on a bench on the back porch of the Math building. He was talking about Swami Vivekananda in a relaxed mood. Incidentally he mentioned an interesting event. One day a young man had come and asked Swami Vivekananda, "Sir, how can one be a successful preacher?" Without saying a word, Swamiji silently passed his right hand from the top of his head over his face, throat and chest down to the navel. The young man was looking at Swamiji and wondered what this meant. Swami Vivekananda asked him, "Do you understand?" "No, Sir," said the young man.

Then Swami Vivekananda passed his hand over his body the same way, as he said, "All these are necessary to be a successful preacher: first of all, the person should have a good brain with the power of sound thinking; next, attractive features; then an eloquent voice; a loving heart; and last but not least is his need of self-control," (while Swamiji's hand reached the navel pointing downward).

One afternoon Swami Premananda wanted me to accompany him while he was going to visit Haramohan Mitra's mother, an old woman who had seen Sri Ramakrishna and was quite devoted to him. Her son, Haramohan, who had passed away some time before, had been a lay disciple of Sri Ramakrishna. It was the mother's influence that had led the son to the feet of the Master.

We crossed the Ganges in a ferry-boat and came to the house where the devout woman lived. She forgot all about her sickness when she saw Swami Premananda, who presented some fruits and vegetables to her, the produce of the Math grounds. We came back to the Math by ferry boat before sunset. It may be noted here that it was Haramohan Mitra who brought out the first Bengali pamphlet on Sri Ramakrishna and his sayings. In this sense he may be counted the pioneer publisher of Ramakrishna literature in Bengali.

During the summer of 1915 when I went to Belur Math, Swami Brahmananda was not there at the time. As far as I know he was staying at Bhadrak (Dist. Balasore, Orissa) in Balaram Bose's estate office building. During this summer vacation it was not possible for me to go to Holy Mother at Jayrambati for initiation. Swami Premananda told me to take a picture of the Holy Mother with me to worship. He sent me to the Udbodhan Office at Baghbazar with a note to Rasbehari Maharaj (Swami Arupananda) asking him to give me a picture of Holy Mother.

In those days Holy Mother's pictures were not offered for sale. This was the first photograph of Holy Mother, taken by the arrangement of Mrs. Sarah Bull, an American disciple of Swami Vivekananda. Holy Mother was then forty-five years of age. I held the picture as a treasure and on my return to Dacca kept it in my shrine along with the picture of Sri Ramakrishna. When I left Dacca for the last time I gave the picture to an earnest devotee.

I also had the privilege of accompanying Swami Premananda to Kalighat, where the temple of the Divine Mother Kali, the presiding deity of the City of Calcutta, is established. Hundreds of pilgrims used to go there daily to offer worship with flowers, fruits, sweets, etc., to the image of the Mother Kali. It was Kiran Chandra Datta, a well-known disciple of Swami Vivekananda and the founder of the Vivekananda Society in Calcutta, who made arrangements for our conveyance. As far as I remember there was another devotee with us younger than myself.

Kiran Datta was a trustee of the estate of the Kali Temple and had great influence over the Temple priests. It was particularly because of this that Swami Premananda and his two young companions had free access to the sanctum sanctorum (Garbha Mandir). As Swami Premananda stood before the image, his face became aglow with divine lustre, his eyes became radiant and even his chest looked ruddy. He was evidently in devotional rapture. I was standing beside him and next to me was the other young man.

At the time of worship or meditation Swami Premananda's countenance glowed with devotion; not only his face and eyes, but his chest also reddened. I had noticed this on more than one occasion. It happened at Belur Monastery every day as he came down the steps after meditation in the shrine. I had the privilege of visiting the temple of the presiding deity of Dacca (Dhakeshwari) with him. There also I noted the same transformation in his features. This testifies to what Sri Ramakrishna said regarding Swami Premananda's intense loving devotion to

God — that it was of the type of Sri Radha's ardent love for God. He further remarked that Baburam was pure to the backbone.

Despite his tender, loving nature Swami Premananda was masculine in his appearance and demeanour. I did not notice any trace of effeminacy in him. His love of God was based on his knowledge of God. Once he asked Sri Ramakrishna for devotional ecstasy. Sri Ramakrishna said he was not meant for that; with love of God he would have knowledge of God, that is, clear perception of spiritual Truth; it was so ordained by the Divine Mother.

On my return to Dacca at the end of the summer vacation in 1915, after living at Belur Monastery in close touch with Swami Premananda, I felt an inner transformation. The significance of the lives and teachings of Sri Ramakrishna and Swami Vivekananda impressed me more deeply than ever before, even though I had been in close touch with the Movement from my early age.

As intended by Swami Vivekananda, Swami Premananda directed his attention specially to East Bengal. "East Bengal is for you," said Swamiji. There was a constant flow of visitors to Belur Math from East Bengal. Being in close touch with the loving spiritual personality of Swami Premananda, many of them became great devotees and admirers of Sri Ramakrishna. Swami Premananda visited East Bengal four times as far as I can recall. A considerable number of young men of the Districts of Dacca and Mymensingh joined the Ramakrishna Order of monks because of the uplifting influence of Swami Premananda's personality. I had the privilege of being with him during his third and fourth visits.

It was in the summer of 1914 that Swami Premananda came to Dacca for the first time after visiting two of the notable villages of East Bengal (Bidgao and Kalma). Some spiritually-minded leaders of the villages had been deeply interested in the teachings of Sri Ramakrishna and Swami Vivekananda. They met the Swami personally at Belur Math and invited him to visit them. At Dacca Swami Premananda stayed in the same Mohini Babu's house where Swami Vivekananda stayed, and where the meetings of the Ramakrishna Association were regularly held. Unfortunately, I was away from the city during his visit which was, however, very short.

The second time, Swami Premananda came to East Bengal towards the end of the spring of 1915, at the cordial invitation of the devotees of Radikhal, and stayed there about two weeks. He and his party were accommodated in the home of the great scientist of international fame, Dr. J. C. Bose. From Radikhal he went back to Belur Math. Not only the Hindu but also the Mohammedan inhabitants of Radikhal and the adjoining villages were deeply influenced by his spiritual personality. His visit left a lasting impression on the minds of all.

It was in January, 1916, that Swami Premananda came to Dacca along with Swami Brahmananda and his party. Besides Swami Brahmananda and Swami Premananda, the party consisted of nine senior and junior sadhus and one devotee of high standing. They came to Dacca after visiting the temple of the Divine Mother at Kamakhya near Gauhati. There the Maharaj performed special worship. On the way they visited Mymensingh at the request of the devotees there. This was Swami Premananda's third visit to East Bengal.

The party arrived at Dacca very late at night by railway train. I was present at the railway station with a landau carriage, drawn by two horses, which belonged to a wealthy friend of mine. I escorted Swami Brahmananda and Swami Premananda to Agnes Villa, where arrangements were made for the accommodation of the entire party. During their stay there I came to see them everyday whenever possible.

One morning I came to Agnes Villa. Just then Swami Premananda happened to come out of the shrine after meditation. His face was radiant with divine lustre. While in this ecstatic mood he saw me, laid his hands upon my shoulders and shook me. I felt blessed.

Swami Brahmananda loved music, particularly devotional songs. In his party there were well-trained singers of devotional songs and expert players on musical instruments in accompaniment. As desired by him, either Ramnama Sankirtanam or Kali Kirtanam was held in chorus regularly in the evening at Agnes Villa for some time during his stay there. These created a holy atmosphere. Swami Brahmananda also told me to join their party.

Swami Brahmananda, Swami Premananda and most of their party once attended the Saturday evening meeting of the Ramakrishna Association at Mohini Babu's house. There were devotional songs, reading of the *Gospel of Sri Ramakrishna,* and a speech by Swami Madhavananda. After the meeting dinner was served to the Swamis and their companions. Jatin Babu was the host. During their stay at Dacca, Maharaj laid the foundation stone of the shrine of the Ramakrishna Math, and Swami Premananda laid the foundation stone of the Ramakrishna Mission building on the permanent site acquired for the purpose. Appropriate ritualistic worship was performed on the occasion.

While at Dacca, Swami Brahmananda and Swami Premananda visited Vijay-krishna Goswami's Ashrama one afternoon with a few attendants. I had the privilege of being in the party. Vijay-krishna Goswami's mother-in-law, who had seen Sri Ramakrishna, was not there at the time. Some of the lay disciples of Vijay-krishna Goswami who lived in the vicinity of the Ashrama came to meet Swami Brahmananda and Swami Premananda on receiving the information. Close to the small brick-built temple, where daily worship was performed, was a small hut with a porch. Maharaj and Swami Premananda took their seats there. After a short conversation both the Swamis were ready to leave. Noticing that the disciples of Vijay-krishna Goswami offered no refreshments to Maharaj, Swami Premananda asked for a glass of water to drink. Glasses of drinking water were offered to them promptly.

This reminded me of what Sri Ramakrishna said about the reception of a holy man visiting a layman's house. In case the host inadvertently offers no food or drink, the holy man should not leave the house without asking just for a glass of water to drink. I had the privilege of seeing Vijay-krishna Goswami's mother-in-law in that Ashrama a few years before Maharaj's visit. I had accompanied an elderly lay disciple of Sri Sarada Devi, the Holy Mother. Vijay-krishna

Goswami's mother-in-law spoke of the three great men she had seen — Sri Ramakrishna Paramahamsa of Dakshineswar, Baba Lokanath Brahmachari of Baradi, and Sri Vijay-krishna Goswami.

From Dacca Maharaj and his party went to Kashimpur at the invitation of Sarada Babu, the owner of Agnes Villa, who usually lived in his country residence. Unfortunately I was not able to join the party.

Swami Brahmananda and Swami Premananda also visited Deobhog, the birthplace of Sadhu Nag Mahasaya. Both of them were in ecstatic moods there. On their way they stopped at Narayangunj. It was not possible for me to undertake this trip because of my mother's illness at the time.

From Dacca Maharaj and his party returned to Belur Math toward the end of February (1916) before Sri Ramakrishna's birth anniversary.

At Dacca I had approached Maharaj (Swami Brahmananda) for spiritual instruction. He told me to wait and see him at Belur Math. Accordingly I came to Belur Math during the summer of 1916. Swami Brahmananda, Swami Premananda, and Swami Shivananda were there at the time. Even though Maharaj agreed to give me spiritual instruction, my mind turned to Holy Mother, who was then at Jayrambati. My plan to go to her for initiation did not, however, succeed. Maharaj graciously gave me instruction preparatory to initiation. I stayed at Belur Math some time longer in association with the three great disciples of Sri Ramakrishna. Swami Shivananda had been at Belur Monastery since spring to relieve the pressure of work on

Swami Premananda.

Swami Brahmananda left for a long trip to Southern India via Madras in July, 1916. Then I came back to Dacca.

Swami Premananda's fourth and final visit to East Bengal was early in the summer of 1917. He came to Dacca after visiting Netrakona in Mymensingh. He stayed for some time at the permanent home of the Ramakrishna Math and Mission, which had been well established by that time. We gathered around him almost everyday. Informal meetings were held in the morning and in the afternoon as well. With his characteristic devotional fervor Swami Premananda usually spoke about Sri Ramakrishna, the Holy Mother and Swami Vivekananda. Visitors increased from day to day.

Once a gentleman who rarely visited the Ashrama came. He requested Swami Premananda to visit his home. Swami Premananda said, "I cannot go by myself, I have to go with the whole party here." Then the gentleman said, "I have a small house and all cannot be accommodated." "In that case you bring your food here. We shall all share it," said Swami Premananda.

One day at Dacca Swami Premananda was invited to a sumptuous feast at the residence of Prafulla Chandra Banerjee, who was a fervent disciple of the Holy Mother and the most enthusiastic member of the local Ramakrishna Math and Mission. The establishment of the permanent home of the Center was considerably due to his earnest efforts. He was a teacher of the Dacca Engineering School. As a Provost of the Students' Hostel, he had spacious living quarters at the entrance to the Hostel compound. All the sadhus of the local Ashrama, many devotees, and some friends of the host participated in the feast.

Before noon the guests were seated in the drawing room of his residence. Swami Premananda was speaking to the group with his usual fervor. Among the audience was the curator of a museum, who was learned and sceptical. He had his seat in front of Swami Premananda. In the course of the talk the Swami said, "Pray to God for spiritual treasures, such as devotion, knowledge, power of discrimination, dispassion, and so forth." Just then the gentleman interrupted: "Why should we pray to God? Does He not know what we need?"

Then the Swami said, "Yes, if you feel that way, if you are convinced that God knows all your needs and will fulfill them, then you need not pray. But many pray to God for the fulfillment of their wordly desires, for material benefits. Is it not wise to pray to Him for the imperishable instead of the perishable? Who but a fool will approach the King of kings for a trifle? If you pray to God, pray to Him for the best."

Then he related the following incident of his early days at Dakshineswar. Hazra Mahasaya was there. He hailed from the same village as Sri Ramakrishna and usually sat on the southeastern verandah of his room, posing as a saintly and learned man. One day he said to Swami Premananda, who was then about nineteen years old, "Well Baburam, why do you not ask Sri Ramakrishna for substantial things? He gives you tid-bits, little delicacies to eat and you are satisfied. You boys are silly. You must secure from him the miraculous powers."

Sri Ramakrishna noticed from his room that Hazra

was whispering something into the ears of young Baburam. When the boy came he wanted to know what Hazra had told him. "He says that I should ask you for substantial things," said the boy. Sri Ramakrishna at once came out of his room and spoke to Hazra, "What is this you teach the boys? Why should they ask me for powers? Do they not know whatever I have is for them? They know their relationship with me. I am their own. They need not ask me for anything."

After recounting the story, Swami Premananda turned to the gentleman and said, "You see, when you know God to be your own and depend on Him completely, then you do not pray to Him for anything."

On several occasions Swami Premananda addressed public meetings. I heard him a few times. Once he was invited to speak before the students in one of the college hostels. He always spoke extemporaneously. Stirring words flowed from the depth of his heart and moved the audience. He stressed the ideal of serving God in man. Any work done in this spirit is veritable worship, as pointed out by Sri Ramakrishna and taught by Swami Vivekananda. To carry into practice the sublime truths of Vedanta is the main objective of the Ramakrishna Math and Mission. Swami Premananda always held this in view and exemplified it in many ways.

Swami Premananda accepted none as a disciple in the strict sense. Whoever approached him for initiation was directed to go to Holy Mother or the Maharaj. Such was his veneration for them that he did not think he should play the role of a guru while they were alive. I knew a school boy who was very eager to receive initiation from Swami Premananda and had looked upon him as his guru for several years. One day at Dacca in our presence he implored the Swami for initiation. We, too, appealed on his behalf. But Swami Premananda was relentless. So with his approval we arranged for the boy's trip to Jayrambati, where he received initiation from Holy Mother.

Though he was reluctant to give initiation, he was ever anxious for the spiritual awakening of all who came to him. By exhortation, by blessing, by touch, by thoughts, by any one or more of these methods, he tried to arouse their dormant spiritual potentialities.

The devotees assembled wherever he went. Not only Hindus of all classes and communities, but Mohammedans also gathered around him. Even persons who were not avowedly religious and who rarely came to the local Ashrama would invariably come to see Swami Premananda when he visited the place. I often wondered who invited them. Besides adults, some young students were drawn to him. Not a few of them entered into monastic life. Their devotional ardor, as far as I know, was mostly the result of their contact with Swami Premananda.

From Dacca Swami Premananda went to Sonargao, a prosperous village not far from Narayangunj (the nearest railway station from Dacca), at the invitation of the founder of the Ashrama there, who was a senior teacher of the local High School. He was a disciple of Holy Mother and very devoted to Swami Premananda. Later he embraced monastic life and became known as Swami Sambuddhananda. He was distinguished in the whole Order for his extraordinary organizing capacity. I was in the party which accompanied Swami Premananda from Dacca. We covered the way by railway train, by steam launch and by boat. The host had made elaborate arrangements for the reception of the Swami and his party on their arrival, for a public meeting on the following day, and for a sumptuous feast.

Shortly after our return to Dacca Swami Premananda was invited to visit some villages not far from the City. It was not possible for me to accompany him on those trips because of previous commitments. Great enthusiasm prevailed wherever Swami Premananda went. Public meetings were held at which he spoke.

He noticed at the same time that the villages were affected by the prevalence of malarial fever, particularly during the rainy season. One of the causes of malarial fever was the lack of pure drinking water. This was due mainly to the luxuriant growth of water hyacinths (Kachuri Pana) in the excavated water tanks, the main source of water in the villages. Noticing the distress of the villagers, ·Swami Premananda urged the young men to organize parties of volunteers to get into the water and remove the water hyacinths. To set an example he himself got into the water to remove some of them. This seriously affected his health.

Shortly after this he returned to Calcutta and became ill of fever. The doctor diagnosed it as Kala-zar. When I came to Calcutta in the autumn of 1917 I saw him bedridden at Balaram Bose's house. I used to see him and inquire about his health as often as possible during my two months' stay at Belur Math and in Calcutta. His condition varied. Unfortunately he did not recover from his illness completely; he passed away in July, 1918.

CHAPTER XII

MEMORIES OF SRI MAHAPURUSHA MAHARAJ[1]
(SWAMI SHIVANANDA)

In getting this opportunity to write down my reminiscences of Mahapurusha Swami Shivananda Maharaj, an apostle and associate of Bhagavan Sri Ramakrishna Deva, and thus being able to meditate on Sri Mahapurushaji, I consider myself blessed. As my sannyasa-guru, he is verily a lighthouse on the path of my life, and is so exemplary as "To be worthy of being remembered the first on waking up in the morning."

Most probably it was during my second visit to the Belur Math, in December, 1911, that I saw Sri Sri Mahapurusha Maharaj for the first time. It was also at the Belur Math, in August of the year 1933, that I saw him last. In the summer of that year I had been on a pilgrimage to the holy Gangotri, Gowmukhi and Jamunotri, with three brother monks of our Order. It was during this sojourn in northern India that we received the news of the serious illness of Mahapurusha Maharaj. We had previously decided to visit Gangotri via Uttarkasi. So as soon as I could at the end of the trip, I left for Belur Math via Kasi to be at the bedside of Mahapurushaji.

Stricken by paralysis and bedridden, he had lost the

[1]English version of the Bengali original, first published in *Vedanta Kesari,* Vol. LVI No. 1, May, 1969, p. 17.
Later published in *Shivananda Smriti Samgraha,* compiled by Swami Apurvananda. Ramakrishna-Shivananda Ashrama, Barasat.

faculty of speech and the right side of his body was completely benumbed. After doing my obeisance I showed him the holy water of the Gowmukhi and the big bark of the birch tree of that region (this bark was formerly used as writing material for manuscripts). With a mute, cheerful face and a compassionate look, he gazed at me, and moving his left arm, blessed me. Then with the help of the attendant he held the vial of the Gowmukhi water on his head and partook of a little of the water. What tremendous devotion and faith he had for the Ganges water and the remains of floral offerings to deities and their prasad! During those days revered Swami Akhandanandaji (Gangadhar Maharaj) was staying at the Belur Math, and upon getting a vial of the Gowmukhi water and a piece of the bark of the birch tree, he too expressed great delight.

In the long course of twenty-two years from December 1911 to August 1933, I had the good fortune of meeting and associating with Mahapurushaji at different times, different places, and in different moods. I met him at Belur Math, at Dakshineswar, at Balaram Mandir, at the Sri Ramakrishna Math at Dacca and at the attached Gaurabash, and at the Sri Ramakrishna Advaita Ashrama in Kasi.

The object of my writing this account is to narrate as faithfully as I can, what I personally saw of him, and what I heard from his holy mouth. Nothing of the miraculous (which is so much relished by ordinary readers) occurred in my presence, and not being in the habit of keeping a diary, I have forgotten many of the incidents. Moreover, for a period of over thirty years I have been residing in America. Nevertheless, I shall try to explain through small incidents and some of his words, how the distinctive inherent nature of Mahapurushaji manifested itself to my mind.

In December, 1911, on the day that I visited the Belur Math for the second time, the most revered Sri Sri Maharaj (Swami Brahmananda) was present there, and of course respected Swami Premananda (Baburam Maharaj) was also there. About four years before, I had the blessed privilege of seeing the two for the first time. My very first visit to the Belur Math was in the month of February, 1908, on the day of the Saraswati Puja. No sooner did I enter the Belur Math than I met Sri Sri Maharaj. From the very beginning I experienced a strong attraction for him because of his compassionate look, affectionate behaviour, and sweet words. Consequently, when I met Sri Sri Maharaj again in 1911, I tried to keep near him as much as possible. Even though I met Sri Sri Mahapurushaji at this time, I did not pay any special attention to him then.

It was in the summer of 1916 at Belur Math that I got the opportunity of coming into close contact with Mahapurushaji. Only a few months before, he had returned to Belur Math after a long sojourn at Almora, Kasi and other places. Because of that sojourn, it had not been possible to see him at Belur Math for a number of years. Within a few days of his return to the Math, he started looking after its activities during the illness of respected Baburam Maharaj.

In those days, the Math library was located in the big room upstairs, to the west of Swamiji's room, in the old Math building. Brahmachari Nagen was the librarian then, and often Swami Vasudevananda used to work with him in the library. During the whitewashing of the room or for some other reason, the books in the library got badly disarranged, so Brahmachari Nagen asked me to check all the books with the catalogue and put them back in order. With much effort I completed the work within two or three days, and gave him a detailed report about the condition of the books. Pleased with this, which was after all a very ordinary piece of work, Mahapurushaji said to me, "Aye, a big work of the Math has been done through you." When I remember his graciousness, he strikes me indeed as "the easily pleased Lord, Ashutosha." (Ashutosha is an epithet of Shiva.)

In those days, Mahapurushaji used to take a walk every afternoon on the grounds by the side of the Ganges. His strides and his movements during his walks appeared regal to us, and the manner in which he shrugged his shoulders everytime he turned depicted his brave nature. On some days I followed him, keeping a respectful distance. One day on meeting a newly-arrived young man he said very gravely, "Remember, you are still under trial." The young man had come from Faridpore, a few days before, with the intention of joining the Order, but he had to go back home within a short time, ordered by the authorities to leave the Math.

Once during the walk I asked Mahapurushaji, "Well, Maharaj. Some take initiation from Sri Sri Ma (the Holy Mother), and others from Maharaj (Swami Brahmananda). Is there any difference between the two?" He said in reply, "No, I do not see any difference whatsoever — the same Ganges water is coming out of two taps. The same grace of Sri Sri Thakur is flowing out through both Ma and

Maharaj; the One Substance is in two receptacles. But look here, what do you mean by '*taking* initiation?' They get it, they get it; it is *given,* it is *given."* No sooner did I hear this than my inner eyes were opened with regard to initiation, and a great problem was solved for me. Dependence on the Divine coupled with self-reliance ruled my heart.

One day at the time of our noon meal together, in the dining hall adjacent to the old kitchen of the Math, Swami Vasudevananda put a question to Sri Mahapurushaji Maharaj. "We have heard that Swamiji gave you the name *Mahapurush.* When and in what circumstance was it given?" Without giving any reply Mahapurushaji sat on, grave.

Then another of the sadhus said, "We have heard that Swamiji and you and Kali Maharaj (Swami Abhedananda) went to Bodh-Gaya a few months before the passing away of Thakur. One night the three of you were immersed in meditation under the Bodhi tree, and Swamiji, imbued with the spirit of Buddha-deva, felt the appearance of Buddha and saw him disappear into your body. From then on, he called you by the name of *Mahapurush."* Mahapurushaji remained quiet. Later he said gravely, "It may be so, or it may be for some other reason."

I concluded from this incident that being designated *Mahapurush* was, so far as he was concerned, quite an insignificant affair. He did not attach any importance to the research into the reasons for this, or it might be that he was not willing to divulge the reason for Swamiji's naming him *Mahapurush.* As far as we know, Mahapurushaji in his youth had to live with his wife under compelling cir-cumstances, but by the especial grace of Sri Sri Thakur, could maintain unbroken celibacy. As soon as Swamiji came to hear of this, he designated Mahapurushaji by that name *(Mahapurush)*.

His greatness and utter unperturbedness can be very clearly seen through a small incident one day. After his meal at night he used to sit, facing the Ganges, on the long bench in the eastern verandah of the ground floor of the old Math building. At the end of talking and smoking, before retiring to bed, he would go for ablution at a fixed spot towards the northwestern corner of the courtyard. One night as he was returning from that spot in the semi-darkness, a youth who was a newcomer to the Math suddenly opened the window on the side of the visitor's room and spat out unawares. At once the youth could very well understand that the whole mouthful of sputum had fallen on the holy body of Mahapurushaji! In an instant, he ran out of the room and fell flat at the feet of Mahapurushaji and begged his pardon.

In no way affected in his mind, Mahapurushaji rinsed himself with some water from the water-bowl in his hand, and assuring the youth of forgiveness and security, said, "Oh, that is nothing, that is nothing. You did not know! It does not matter at all! Go, go." In fact he showed an attitude which suggested that the offense of the young man was not even so serious as to need any begging for forgiveness. But the young man could not easily forget his offense. Only by relying on the grace of Mahapurushaji, which flowed spontaneously without cause and reason, did he derive consolation.

One of the inherent qualities of Mahapurushaji was that he looked upon all in a magnanimous way. Coming into contact with him I became convinced of the fact that to judge people by means of their faults was the habit of smaller folk, but to judge others by means of their good qualities was the way of noble men. Mahapurushaji would not easily give ear to an accusation against anyone. Even if an abuse did fall on his ears he would not give it a place in his mind, and it would leave no trace of an imprint there. Sometimes he would say, "No, no. I know he is a good boy." Even when one of the monks of the organization had committed a grave offense, it was very difficult for the elder sadhus of the Order to convince Mahapurushaji of it. When I remember the magnanimity of Mahapurushaji I am many times reminded of the following verse in Bhartrihari's *Nitisataka* (One hundred verses on Ethics and Morals):

> How few noble spirits there are whose thoughts, speech and actions are, so to speak, impregnated with nector; by whom countless blessings are bestowed upon the three worlds; who exalt even the slightest virtues of another to the height of a mountain, and whose hearts are continually overflowing!

For a long time, I had heard about the indifferent and disregarding attitude of Mahapurushaji to people in general. But from the very beginning, he treated me like an old acquaintance of his, and always looked upon me with affectionate eyes. The main reason for this was his innately affectionate nature. The example of an exceedingly soft heart, able to function within the dry sternness of the anchorite, was always seen manifested in his life and behaviour —he had deep love and reverence for his brother-disciples. Because I could earlier earn the compassion and affection of Sri Sri Maharaj and Baburam Maharaj, the compassionate and affectionate eyes of Mahapurushaji easily fell on me. All along I had noticed his natural affection, especially for those who were the recipients of the grace of Sri Sri Maharaj.

Besides this, Mahapurushaji knew that I had had the great good fortune to see revered Swamiji at the start of my student life, in 1901, and that from a few years after that I had been engaged in building my life in accordance with the teachings of Sri Sri Thakur and Swamiji. I had been busy in organizing religious conferences, and running institutions of service. He considered leading even this type of life an austerity, and now and then would mention it to others. It was his firm conviction that no great work could be successful without austerity, and that the fruit of religious austerity was bound to come.

At the bidding of Sri Sri Maharaj I served my mother very earnestly as long as she was alive. On her demise in 1924 I wrote to Mahapurushaji, begging initiation into sannyas. Without delay, he expressed his willingness to give me sannyas in a letter written in his own hand. But as ill-luck would have it, I could not be so initiated on the birthday of Sri Sri Thakur in 1925. Hence he initiated me into Brahmacharya with the sacred thread and ochre robe, and later, in 1927, at the holy pilgrim-centre of Kasidham on the birthday of Sri Sri Ma, he initiated me into sannyas.

I shall mention here one instance of the affectionate nature of Mahapurushaji. A few years after this, I returned to Belur Math and went to his room in the morning to pay my respects to him. When I had saluted him and he had inquired about my health and welfare, he called the storekeeper of the Math in my very presence, and arranged regular meals for me in such a way as to aid my healthful living.

Sri Sri Maharaj once wrote a letter to Mahapurushaji in amusement and fun. The incident may appear insignificant in itself, but it reveals what a sweet relationship there was between the two, and helps us understand their deep, abiding affection and friendship.*

One day at the beginning of the winter season in 1917, in the drawing room of Balaram Mandir, Maharaj asked me to bring him pen, ink and a piece of writing paper. When he began to dictate in English, I took down what he said. Now and then he told me to make the necessary corrections in the language. He dictated at one place, "will be successful." With his permission I wrote, "will be crowned with success." The letter was addressed, "To the Abbot, Belur Monastery." At the time, Mahapurushaji was in charge at the Belur Math, as respected Baburam Maharaj was lying ill in the small room adjoining the Balaram Mandir.

The gist of the letter was: "The Christmas celebration will surely be observed at your Math. On that occasion we — a party of monks — are coming to the Math. Your hospitality is well-known. Certainly at the conclusion of the ceremony, according to the usual custom in Christmas celebrations, there will be an arrangement for the taking of drinks. We are non-vegetarians and are fond of varied courses of meat dishes. In anticipation of a sumptuous feast,

*This same incident has been related in an earlier chapter in my reminiscences of Swami Brahmananda.

we extend to you our heartfelt thanks. May your function be crowned with success in all possible ways; that is our earnest wish."

When I had written the letter I handed it to him for his signature, but instead of putting his own name, he signed "Premananda" and told me, "Go and read the letter to Baburam Maharaj." Hearing the contents of the letter and finding his signature forged, Baburam Maharaj simply smiled, and said, "Maharaj has a child-like nature." One thing has to be especially noted here — both Baburam Maharaj and Mahapurushaji were vegetarians.

Later Maharaj asked me to go to Belur Math and deliver the letter to Mahapurushaji, but cautioned me not to mention that he had sent it. After reading through the letter, Mahapurushaji looked at me and said laughing, "Maharaj has sent this. Is that not so?" Without a word I nodded my head a little. Mahapurushaji understood, "Silence is acquiescence."

The following instance comes to my mind of the vision with which Mahapurushaji looked upon the monks of the Order. In 1926, a convention of all the Ramakrishna Math and Mission centres was held at Belur Math. Mahapurushaji as the President and Swami Saradananda as the Secretary addressed the assembly, and Swami Paramananda came from America to take part in the convention.

As far as I can recollect, after the convention in the month of May in the dense darkness of a new moon night, the worship of Mother Kali was performed at the Math. With the permission of Mahapurushaji, Swami Omkarananda (Ananga Maharaj) began the worship at the beginning of the night. Without any assistance from the Tantradhar (Prompter) he completed the puja himself, performing the many details one by one throughout the night.

In the morning, after meeting and saluting Sri Sri Mahapurushaji, I said, "Ananga Maharaj is an adept in the art of worship. Single-handed he completed the whole of the puja, without leaving his seat the entire night. He is very well-trained!" Smiling, Mahapurushaji replied, "Not only in this birth! It is the fruit of spiritual practices in other and previous births. None can come into the circle of Thakur without the merit of the good deeds of the past and bygone births. Know that they who have arrived and collected at the door of Thakur are highly virtuous and righteous people."

Mahapurushaji was very able to get at the spirit of a thing. During the early part of the year 1923, while staying at the Dacca Ramakrishna Math, he was present one day at Gaurabash at one of the weekly sittings of the association. I was to read the *Katha Upanishad* to the assembly that day. I read (along with their rendering in Bengali) the two verses which say:

> Know the Self as the rider and the Body as the Chariot. Know the Intelligence as the driver and the Mind as the rein. The knowers call the Senses the horses, and call the Objects of sense-enjoyment the paths for the movement of horses, and they call the Soul, conjoined with the sense-organs and the mind, the Enjoyer.   (Ka.U. I:iii:3-4)

After the reading there was a short explanation and a discussion. Mahapurushaji listened, keeping silent, and later said, "Look here. The Self is body-transcending, undecaying, Immortal; Pure-Eternal-Free in essence — if this conviction is got, the purpose of the study of the *Upanishads* is gained. The next step is to get Self-knowledge —through religious discipline and devotion; this is the whole of the matter."

I noticed that same day the great control Mahapurushaji had over his diet. Arrangements had been made for his dinner after the assembly at Gaurabash had met and dispersed. The dinner was laid on a large table of white marble in the drawing room on the first floor of the inner apartment. It consisted of various dishes kept in several small receptacles. Devoted women-neighbours had brought many different items of food and sweets, prepared by their own hands. Mahapurushaji took his seat on a chair to take his dinner. Touching them only with his forefinger, one by one he put each of the several items of food on his tongue and repeatedly said, "Good, good. Very tasteful! Very delicious!" But he did not taste any of the items a second time. As far as I know, the daily menu of his diet consisted principally of decoction-like soup and ordinary cooked rice, and for sweets a little sandesh.

Once at the Dacca Math on being questioned about the samadhi of Sri Sri Thakur, he replied, "During samadhi the countenance of Thakur would beam bright with Self-effulgence and Bliss [*Atmajyoti* and *Ananda*]. Nitygopal also used to get Bhava-samadhi, but on seeing him it struck one that he was joyless within, as though in great pain."

At Dacca, responding to the deep eagerness of many initiation-seekers, and because of the pressing request of the head of the Dacca Math, Mahapurushaji agreed to give initiation. But prior to doing so he had written to Sri Sri Maharaj, the President of the Order, seeking his permission. In reply to the letter, Maharaj sent a telegram and with much insistence urged Mahapurushaji to give initiation. Before then Mahapurushaji had never given initiation to anyone. As far as I know, on some occasions he had instructed a few persons regarding spiritual practice and devotion.

Within a very short time after this, he received telegraphic information about the serious illness of Sri Sri Maharaj. Greatly worried about Maharaj, without any delay Mahapurushaji returned to Calcutta and reached Balaram Mandir to be by his bedside. He remained there to the last moments of Maharaj.

On the birthday of Sri Sri Mahapurushaji in 1927, his widowed sister, who was at the time in Kasi, came to the Advaita Ashrama there and spent nearly the entire day. Most probably Swami Nirbharananda (Chandra Baba), the Monk-in-charge of the Advaita Ashrama, had asked her to come. In his conversations and behaviour with his sister, Mahapurushaji exhibited no special delight or intentness, and no indifference or discourtesy. I observed with particular attention his self-possession and composure. When I think of it, this sloka in the *Gita* comes to my mind:

Even here is the relative existence conquered by them whose mind rests in equality; for Brahman is even and faultless, therefore are they established in Brahman. (5:19)

At the bidding of Mahapurushaji I took charge of the Ashrama at Delhi and worked there for almost six years (1931-1936). It is my conviction that whatever success was achieved in the work there was due to his blessings. At the great insistence and earnest request of Swami Sharvanandaji I left Mayavati Ashrama and came to Delhi; the Ashrama there was then located in a rented building in old Delhi. I found the condition of the Ashrama such that I did not feel at all like staying there.

Swami Shuddhanandaji had also come, and had been staying at the Delhi Ashrama for a few days. Both he and Swami Sharvananda asked me insistently to take charge of the work there. Without consenting to be there under any circumstances, I returned to Belur Math. Swami Sharvananda wrote to Mahapurushaji at Belur strongly urging him to send me to Delhi. Mahapurushaji asked me, explaining the situation in various ways, to proceed to Delhi. Bowing to his order, with due submission I went to Delhi.

Those were the days of the British rule, and some time before, the British Indian Government had allotted a plot for the Ashrama. In giving possession of the land; in enclosing the plot by boundary walls; in putting up quarters; in taking up residence there — in everyone of these things difficulties were created. The main reasons for this state of affairs were the petty outlook of some Government employees, the rigid rules and regulations, and the antagonism of others.

Without being down-hearted in any way, I tried to meet every situation with unflagging zeal according to the demands of the occasion. Not even for a day did I feel any despair or exhaustion though now and then some of the well-wishers and friends of the Ashrama would feel despondent. Slowly but steadily, all the obstacles were removed and the Ashrama was established on a firm footing. Some of the most intricate problems were resolved in amazing ways, and Divine dispensation seems to have been the only explanation for it.

The chief characteristic of Mahapurushaji seemed to be that his life was immersed in Sri Sri Thakur; Mahapurushaji was the very personification of self-surrender to the Divine. Once during the summer, I came to the Math from Delhi. When I met an elder sannyasin he told me, "These days a manifestation of wonderful power is seen in Mahapurushaji. Drawn from far-off places by his great attraction, high-placed persons, respectable and noble ladies and gentlemen, and even Rajas and Ranis, are coming to the Math for his audience." I heard all this in mute wonder.

Just after this I went to meet Mahapurushaji, who was resting after his mid-day meal on the eastern verandah in the upper story of the old building of the Math. He was sitting on a chair, facing the Ganges with his two feet placed on his slippers which were on the floor. After prostrating myself I sat on the floor, gazing at him. No other person was present. Before I could speak, Mahapurushaji looked at me and said, "Just see, this is the condition of the body! Shattered! It is all right one day and is ailing the next day. See, Thakur is sporting with this! Our Thakur is an adept player! He wins the game with even a bad coin [pointing to his body]." I began to think, "Bad coin, indeed!"

Having surrendered body, mind and soul to Thakur Sri Ramakrishna, Mahapurushaji had become Thakur-all-over.

VEDANTA IN AMERICA

"How does the Vedanta mission in the United States differ from the Christian missions in India?"

The above question was asked by a member of a prominent church in the St. Louis area on January 7, 1957, at the Vedanta Society of St. Louis. Swami Satprakashananda, the head of the Society, gave the following reply:

I cannot say anything about the present Christian missionary activities in India, since I have had no direct knowledge of them for many years. I can only tell you of our ideas and methods of work in the United States.

It is to be noted that Vedanta is not an exclusive religion. It holds fast to the universal spiritual truths which underlie all religious doctrines and disciplines. As such, it is the common basis, the foundation of all religions.

We do not inculcate dogmas or creeds. We deal particularly with spiritual principles and practices common to most religions. We give a rational explanation of what we teach. Consequently, our teachings appeal to men and women irrespective of race, nationality, or religious persuasion.

In the light of Vedantic teachings, the followers of different religions have a better understanding of their respective religions, and of other religions as well. Our ministry is twofold: to help individuals to develop spiritually, and to promote mutual understanding and appreciation among the followers of different religions. Persons belonging to any religion can receive our help without changing their faith; we accept all religions as pathways to God.

We worship Jesus Christ as one of the saviors. In fact, we believe in all the great founders of religions.

We seek no converts. We want to see that our students and members strive after spiritual living, regardless of what they call themselves — Christians, Vedantists, Jews, or Hindus.

Our work is intended to make a Christian a better Christian, a Jew a better Jew, a Mohammedan a better Mohammedan, a Hindu a better Hindu. Through our teachings many who were born in Christian families, but had no faith in Christianity, have gained faith in their religion.

We see no difference between a true Christian and a true Hindu, so far as the spiritual life is concerned. One is as near God as the other. If we approach the sun along different radii, we come closer to one another as we near it too.

The Vedantic teaching that man can attain complete self-fulfillment by realizing God provides seekers with the meaning of life. It fuses hope in the non-believers, as it confirms the believers.

Vedanta stresses the need of moral values for material well-being, and points out that man's moral life rests on a spiritual foundation. Thus, while developing man's spiritual nature, Vedanta promotes peace, progress, and security in individual and collective life. Our teachings find access to human hearts because of their intrinsic value.

We disseminate spiritual and ethical ideas and ideals without persuasion or pressure. We are not sent from India as missionaries, but come on invitation from individuals or groups interested in Vedanta.

We are not professionals or careerists, but monastic teachers living consecrated lives. We receive no salary, but depend on voluntary contributions. Our work is financed solely by our American students and friends.

We take no part in politics or social organizations. Our work does not create a cleavage — cultural, national, or social — between the Vedanta group and any other section of people. We do not carry on any social service with the idea of proselytization.

The teachings of Vedanta are spreading in America slowly but steadily. The work was started by Swami Vivekananda sixty-four years ago [1893]. At present there are about a dozen Vedanta Centers in the United States, each under a monastic teacher of the Ramakrishna Order.

RAMAKRISHNA MATH AND THE
NON-DUALISTIC ORDER OF SHANKARA

It may be noted in this context that the monks of the Ramakrishna Order formally belong to the same order of sannyasins which was established by Shankaracharya, the greatest advocate of nondualistic Vedanta, early in the eighth century, A.D. Shankara reorganized the ancient monastic order under ten different denominations: Giri, Puri, Bharati, Saraswati, Bana, Aranya, Tirtha, Ashrama, Parbata, and Sagara. Tota-puri, who initiated Sri Ramakrishna into sannyasa and guided him to the realization of nondual Brahman in nirvikalpa samadhi, belonged to the Puri class.

Shankara also founded four principal monasteries at the four cardinal points of India. Near the temple of Rameswara Shiva at the southwest point of India he founded the Sringeri Math; at Puri on the Bay of Bengal in the east he founded the Govardhan Math; at Dwarka on the Arabian Sea in the west he founded Sarada Math; and in the north on the Himalayan heights, Jyotir Math at Joshi, adjacent to Badarika Ashrama.

Each of Shankara's four main disciples took charge of one of the monasteries. Suresharacharya took charge of Sringeri Math in the south; Padmapadacharya of the Govardhan Math at Puri; Hastamalaka of the Sarada Math at Dwarka; and Totakacharya of the Jyotir Math at Joshi in the Himalayas.

For special study, each of the four monasteries took charge of one of the four Vedas — Rig, Yajur, Sama, Atharva. Govardhan Math became custodian of the Rig Veda; Sringeri Math of the Yajur Veda; Sarada Math of the Sama Veda; and Jyotir Math of the Atharva Veda. The head of each of the monasteries was to promote by example and by precept the spiritual well-being of the laity as well as of the monastics.

Since Tota-puri, monastic guru of Sri Ramakrishna, belonged to Sringeri Math in the south, consequently the monks of the Ramakrishna Order initiated by Sri Ramakrishna and organized by Swami Vivekananda belong to the Puri Order of Sannyasins. They owe allegiance to Sringeri Math in southwest India, the custodian of the Yajur Veda, to which the Brihadaranyaka Upanishad belongs. Monastics of the Ramakrishna Order are esteemed by the sannyasins of the ancient nondualistic order established by Shankaracharya, and are invited to their feasts and other special functions.

SRI RAMAKRISHNA'S MESSAGE OF RENUNCIATION AND REALIZATION IN TERMS OF VEDANTA

Once a well-to-do person came to a holy man who was living under a tree with no belongings except for two pieces of blanket and a loincloth. The gentleman was praising the holy man for his renunciation. But the holy man replied, "you are a man of greater renunciation than I am; because I have renounced the ephemeral, the unreal, for the sake of the Real. But you have renounced the Real for the sake of the unreal."

Through the sacred order of sannyas, the life of renunciation has existed in India from time immemorial in an unbroken line of teachers and disciples. It is a life of consecration to God, and service of God in man. In one sense it is complete renunciation of the world; in another sense it is whole-hearted acceptance of the Divine Being, who is the one source of all life, all knowledge, all love, all joy, and all blessedness. It is abandonment of the transitory for the sake of the eternal.

An important function of the ceremony of sannyas is that at the time of initiation the teacher imparts to the disciple a terse formula by which the initiate tries to fix his mind on the Supreme Being. This precept is the very essence of spiritual knowledge. It furnishes the key to the spiritual life of man, and presents in a nutshell the Vedantic view of

God, the Vedantic view of man, the Vedantic view of man's approach to God, and the Vedantic view of the other religions of the world.

This pithy sentence is called *mahavakya,* the great saying. The entire Vedic literature is an amplification of this supreme teaching. In each of the four Vedas there is such a saying.

In the Aitareya Upanishad, which belongs to the Rig Veda, this truth is expressed as "Consciousness is Brahman." It means that the individual consciousness, the center of the human personality, is no different from the Supreme Consciousness that manifests and sustains the universe.

In the Brihadaranyaka Upanishad, which belongs to the Yajur Veda, this same truth is presented in the form: "I am Brahman." Here "I" means not the physical or psychophysical "I," but the real "I," the spiritual Self that dwells in the psychophysical system, that integrates all the psychical and the physical elements into a coherent whole. The individual soul is essentially the same as the Supreme Self, the all-pervading Being.

In the Chandogya Upanishad, which belongs to the Sama Veda, this teaching is imparted as "That Thou Art." The Supreme Being, which is usually conceived as the farthest, as the most inaccessible, as that which is beyond the reach of the senses and the mind, is the very essence of the universe, the fundamental Reality underlying all transitory forms. "That" is the indwelling Self within each and every individual being.

This instruction, "That Thou Art," was given by the

sage Uddalaka to his son Svetaketu. But the son did not understand. Uddalaka and Svetaketu were standing near a huge Nyagrodha tree (probably a tree of the fig family), and the father told his son to bring a fruit of this tree.

"Here is the fruit," said the son. "Please break it," said the father.

"It is broken, sir." "What do you find?"

"Innumerable tiny seeds." "Please break one of the seeds."

"It is broken, sir." "What do you see?"

"Nothing, sir."

"My child, what you do not see is the very essence which makes the tree germinate, develop, and by which it is sustained. Similarly, that subtle essence which is imperceptible to the senses, which is incomprehensible even to the mind, is the all-pervading Reality which produces, supports, and sustains the universe. That dwells within you as your inner-most Self."

In the Mandukya Upanishad, which belongs to the Atharva Veda, this truth is given in another form: "This Self is Brahman." It removes completely man's misconception regarding himself and God. Man is not a physical or a psychophysical being. He knows the body, the senses, and the mind, and rules over them. As the knowing Self, he is the conscious spirit, ever pure, free, and luminous.

Apparently he is mortal, but actually he is immortal; apparently he is bound, but actually he is free; apparently he is imperfect, but actually he is perfect; apparently he is human, but actually he is divine.

Being falsely identified with the body, the senses, and

the mind, man ascribes to himself birth, growth, decay, death, hunger, thirst, pain, pleasure, virtue, vice, knowledge, and ignorance. The real Self, which sees through the eyes, hears through the ears, works through the hands, speaks through the mouth, knows through the mind, is not limited by the psychophysical system, but is identical with the all-pervading Supreme Being, who is self-luminous, being of the nature of Pure Consciousness.

We live in Him, we move in Him, we have our being in Him; still we are unaware of Him. Just as blind people living and moving in the full splendor of sunlight cannot perceive it, similarly we fail to perceive that self-effulgent One because of our inner blindness. The moment the veil of darkness drops from our inner eye we realize That.

This experience has been testified to in the life of Sri Ramakrishna in this modern age. He realized Supreme Consciousness as shining through each and every thing he saw: through the temple, through the doors, through the utensils with which the worship of the Divine Being was performed.

God is not an extra-cosmic Being far away from us. What can be nearer than the innermost Self? That which seems to be the most remote is the closest of all. That which seems to be inaccessible is already attained. That which seems to be hidden is self-manifest. Consequently, the way to God-realization is an inner approach. To reach the soul of the universe, you must reach your own soul. You contact Supreme Spirit through spirit. As Sri Ramakrishna says, *"Bodhe bodh,"* that is, one communes with the Supreme Consciousness through the inner consciousness. There cannot be a more direct instruction regarding the Supreme Being than to declare Him the innermost Self of man.

The sacred formula "I am Brahman" is resolved into two factors: "I am He," and "I am His." The first means that the individual self is identical with the Supreme Self. This constitutes the direct approach to the Impersonal Absolute Being, (Nirguna Brahman). It is a very steep course and is technically called the path of knowledge.

The other factor, "I am His," is the approach to the Personal God (Saguna Brahman) through the consciousness of the relationship between Him and the individual self. This is the path of devotion. It forms the basis of all the theistic religions of the world.

The relationship between God and man assumes different forms in different religions. In some it is manifest particularly as the relationship between the master and the servant, in some as the relationship between the ruler and the ruled, in some as that between the parent and the child, and so forth. Thus each of these terse formulas: "Consciousness is Brahman," "I am Brahman," "That Thou Art," "This Self is Brahman," covers the entire religious life of man. This is the key to God-realization.

The same reality, Pure Consciousness, has different aspects in relation to the universe. As the transcendent Being beyond all distinctions and differences, beyond the dualities of good and evil, of pain and pleasure, of life and death, it is Brahman. As immanent in the universe it is Paramatman, the Supreme Self. As the Ruler of the universe it is Ishwara, the Supreme Lord. As the Leader of all souls, as the Giver of Liberation, it is Bhagavan, the God of love and grace, worshiped by the devotees. The same nondual Consciousness is the indwelling Self of each and every individual. What is innermost in the universe is innermost in each and every one of us.

All that a person has to do is to turn the mind toward the Supreme Being. The more the mind is turned toward the Supreme Being, the purer it becomes; because He is the holiest of the holy, the Light of all lights. One can turn the mind to the Supreme Being through work, or through devotional worship, or through meditation, or through discrimination.

The more the mind is purified, the more the light of the Supreme Being shines from within. By constantly dwelling on the Supreme Being, the mind, when it is completely purified, becomes tranquil and transparent and suffused with the Divine Consciousness. This is how God is realized.

Sri Ramakrishna refers to this inner approach when he says, "A man can know God if he can know himself." In trying to find your real Self you find God! It is this very teaching which has been given first place in the *Words of the Master,* compiled by Swami Brahmananda.

"The Kingdom of God is within you," says Jesus Christ. Turn your thoughts inward, receive the light of the indwelling Spirit by whatever spiritual discipline you can practice, until you realize Him as the Soul of your soul. This is the way to freedom, this is the way to absolute peace and blessedness.

THE MASTER'S SELF-REVELATION AND THE BESTOWAL OF FREEDOM FROM FEAR[1]
Recorded by Swami Saradananda

It was the first day of January, 1886 A.D. As the Master felt somewhat well that day, he expressed a desire to come out of his room and have a walk in the garden for some time. It was a holiday and the householder devotees came one by one and in groups shortly after midday. Thus when the Master came downstairs at three in the afternoon, more than thirty people were engaged in conversation in the garden under the trees, or inside the house.

As soon as they saw him, all got up out of reverence and bowed down to him. He came down to the garden path through the western door of the hall on the ground floor, and was slowly proceeding southward to the gate when all followed him at a little distance. When he came to the middle of the path leading to the gate, he saw Girish, Ram, Atul and a few others, sitting under the trees to the west of the path. They also saw him, and saluted him from there and came joyfully to him.

The Master addressed Girish all of a sudden before anybody had spoken a word, and said, "Girish — you, I find, say to one and all everywhere so many things about me (that

[1]Saradananda, S., *Sri Ramakrishna The Great Master,* pp. 889-92. Mylapore-Madras: 1952.
Reprinted here on the event's 90th anniversary, January 1, 1976.

I am an incarnation of God); what have you seen and understood (about me) that you do so?"

Girish remained completely unmoved, and kneeling down on the ground near the Master's feet, said in a choked voice with his hands folded and face upwards, "What more can I say of Him, Whose greatness Vyasa and Valmiki [authors of the *Brahma Sutras* and *Ramayana,* respectively] could not find words to express?"

The Master was charmed at this fervent utterance of the devoted Girish, and blessed all the devotees assembled there through their representative Girish: "What more shall I say to you? May you all be blessed with the spiritual awakening." Beside himself with love and compassion for the devotees, hardly had he said those few words when he entered into Bhavasamadhi.

Those words of profound blessing, untouched by the slightest tinge of selfishness, directly entered the devotees' hearts where they raised high billows of bliss. They forgot time and space, forgot the disease of the Master and forgot their previous determination not to touch him till he recovered, and were aware only that out of sympathy for them in their plight, an extraordinary diving Being, feeling excruciating pain at their misery and his heart overflowing with compassion, had come down to them from heaven and called them affectionately to Him for protection, like a mother sheltering her children against all ills by covering them lovingly with the upper part of her sari.

They then became eager to bow down to him and take the dust of his feet, and filling the quarters with cries of "Victory to Ramakrishna," began saluting him one after another. As they were thus bowing down to him, the sea of the Master's compassion transcended all bounds and brought about a wonderful phenomenon.

We had almost daily seen the Master at Dakshineswar losing himself in grace and compassion for certain devotees, and blessing them by his extraordinary potent touch in the state of divine semi-consciousness. He began touching each of the devotees assembled on that day in that divine mood. The joy of the devotees, it is superfluous to say, knew no bounds at that act of the Master.

They felt that he would not henceforward keep concealed the fact of his divinity either from them or from anybody else in the world; and knowing, as they did, nevertheless, their own defects, spiritual destitution and incapability, they had not the slightest doubt that all alike, the sinner and the afflicted, would find a refuge at his feet, a touch of which dispelled all fear forever.

Unable to utter a single word owing to that wonderful happening, some were only looking steadfastly at him as if they were under the spell of a mantra, some others called aloud to all within the house to come and be blessed by receiving the Master's grace, and still others collected flowers, and worshipped him with them uttering mantras.

Soon the ecstasy of the Master came to an end and the devotees too were in the normal state of their consciousness. Bringing thus to an end his walk in the garden that day, he went into the house and sat down in his room.

Some devotees like Ramchandra have described the happening of that day as the transformation by the Master of himself into the wish-fulfilling tree (Kalpataru). But it is more reasonable, it seems to us, to call it 'the self-revelation of the Master,' or the 'bestowal of freedom from fear on all devotees by revealing himself.' The Kalpataru, it is said, gives to all whatever good or bad they ask for.

But the Master did not do so; he made clear through that event the fact of his being a God-man, and of his bestowal of protection against and freedom from fear on all without the slightest discrimination.

Be that as it may, of all the people that felt blessed by having his grace on that day, Haranchandra Das is worthy of being particularly mentioned. For as soon as he bowed down to him, the Master in Bhavasamadhi placed his lotus feet on Haran's head. It is only on a few occasions that we saw him bestow his grace in this way.

Ramlal Chattopadhyaya was present there on that occasion and also received the Master's grace. Asked about it, he said, "I could formerly see a part only of the holy person of my chosen Ideal with my mind's eye at the time of meditation — when I saw the lotus feet, I could not see the face; again perhaps I saw the person from the face to the waist, but could not see the holy feet, and whatever I saw never seemed to be alive — but no sooner had the Master touched me that day than the form of my chosen Ideal with all the limbs appeared suddenly from head to foot in the lotus of my heart and moved and looked benign and effulgent."

We remember the names of nine or ten only of the persons who were present on the spot of this day's occurrence. They are Girish, Atul, Ram, Navagopal, Haramohan, Vaikuntha, Kishori (Roy), Haran, Ramlal and

Akshay. Mahendranath, (the writer of the *Gospel of Sri Ramakrishna),* perhaps was also present.

But it is a matter of wonder that none of the Sannyasi [monastic] devotees of the Master was present there that day. Narendranath and many others of them had been engaged in sadhana besides the Master's service, etc., in the previous night for long hours, and feeling tired they were sleeping within the house.

Although Latu and Sarat [later Swamis Adbhutananda and Saradananda] were awake and saw what was taking place from the roof of the first floor to the south of the Master's room, they refrained voluntarily from going there. For as soon as the Master went downstairs to have a walk in the garden, they put his beddings, etc., in the sun and were cleaning the room. Thinking that it might cause inconvenience to the Master if they left their duty half-finished, they did not feel inclined to go there.

INDEX